Strength and Longevity: Building Muscle After 50 Isn't Optional—It's Survival

SOUTHERLAND | COPYRIGHT 2025

Contents

Chapter 1: The Muscle Cliff After 50

By the time most people reach their early fifties, the physiological undercurrent pulling them toward weakness is already well underway. Sarcopenia, the age-related loss of muscle mass and strength, doesn't announce itself with sirens or alarms. It begins subtly—slight reductions in grip strength, longer recovery times from physical tasks, and a growing reluctance to carry groceries in one trip. This isn't just middle-aged inconvenience; it is the biological equivalent of walking toward a cliff with poor lighting and no guardrails. Most won't notice until they're mid-air. Research shows that muscle mass declines at a rate of approximately 1% per year after the age of 50, and strength diminishes even faster—up to 3% annually. That means within a decade, even relatively active individuals can lose a third of their muscular strength if they aren't actively resisting the process. The term "active" here is deceptive. Walking, gardening, even frequent cycling aren't enough. This cliff cannot be scaled by casual motion; it requires resistance.

This rapid descent isn't just about aesthetics or diminished gym performance. The loss of lean muscle accelerates every other marker of decline. Muscle tissue is metabolically active—it supports glucose regulation, thermogenesis, mobility, and hormonal stability. As it erodes, the entire system begins to destabilize. Fat mass increases not solely because of overeating but because the body's resting energy demands drop. Insulin sensitivity wanes because muscle, the primary site for glucose disposal, is no longer available to soak up circulating sugar. Balance falters because the neuromuscular coordination once reinforced by loaded movement starts to decay. What appears on the surface as "just getting older" is often just unchecked muscle loss manifesting in diverse and catastrophic ways.

Sarcopenia has become so normalized in modern aging that most people—and, crucially, many physicians—accept it as inevitable. Yet it is neither normal nor inevitable in the evolutionary sense. Pre-industrial populations retained muscular competence into old age because their lifestyles demanded it. The human body doesn't deteriorate from age alone; it deteriorates from disuse. Biologically, we are not programmed to fall apart at 50—we are programmed to adapt to stress. When mechanical loading stops, adaptation reverses. Studies of master athletes—those who have continued resistance or power training into their 60s and 70s—consistently show muscle cross-sectional area, mitochondrial density, and strength metrics far superior to those of sedentary peers, even when matched for age. The divergence isn't genetic; it's behavioral.

This is not to romanticize aging or suggest invincibility through iron. Age still matters. Protein synthesis rates slow with age, recovery windows lengthen, and anabolic resistance—the body's blunted muscle-building response to stimuli—grows more stubborn. However, these shifts don't create the cliff; they merely steepen the slope. Without countermeasures, even minor strength deficits compound rapidly. A reduction in quadriceps strength, for instance, correlates directly with slower gait speed, which in turn predicts mortality risk. Declining grip strength is linked with higher incidence of hospitalization, disability, and all-cause death—so much so that it is now considered a biomarker in several aging studies. Yet no one tells you this at your annual physical. You'll get blood drawn for cholesterol, but no one will test how much weight your legs can push.

The invisibility of sarcopenia in mainstream health discourse compounds its danger. Bone density has advocates—DEXA scans, osteoporosis commercials, calcium supplements with glossy labels. But muscle mass? It suffers from a PR problem. You lose it gradually, and then suddenly. A moment comes—stepping off a curb awkwardly, missing a stair, trying to lift a suitcase—when the deficit announces itself in stark clarity. The fall happens not because of a specific injury, but because of years of accumulated inaction. Most people who enter hospitals after a fall don't leave more mobile; nearly half experience long-term functional loss. This is what the muscle cliff looks like in practice: one moment of instability followed by a permanent reduction in independence.

By the time individuals realize the seriousness of muscle loss, they often assume it's too late. This belief is as destructive as the loss itself. Numerous trials have shown that resistance training is effective even in the eighth and ninth decades of life. A 2020 meta-analysis published in *Ageing Research Reviews* found significant gains in strength and muscle mass among people aged 70 and older who began progressive resistance training protocols. The mechanism of adaptation doesn't switch off—it just requires a louder signal. For older adults, that means more intentional training with appropriate volume, intensity, and recovery. The response may be slower, but it remains potent.

Despite this, many over-50 adults avoid resistance training due to misconceptions about injury risk, complexity, or vanity. The irony is that avoiding load is precisely what guarantees decline.

While poor programming or overzealous lifting can indeed cause injury, properly structured strength training is statistically safer than most recreational sports. The most common "injury" from resistance training after 50 isn't a torn muscle—it's sore pride from realizing how much strength has already slipped away. That discomfort, however, is useful. It creates awareness. And awareness is the first prerequisite for adaptation.

Another reason the cliff remains unspoken is cultural. In Western societies, muscle is still coded as a symbol of youth, vanity, or performance. Older individuals are subtly discouraged from lifting with intensity. Fitness marketing for seniors emphasizes light weights, bands, and "functional" movement as euphemisms for de-training. This soft approach is not just ineffective; it is actively harmful. Functional movement is built on strength. Without force output, movement patterns degrade regardless of mobility drills or balance work. The ability to rise from a chair without using hands, to climb stairs without bracing on the rail, or to carry one's own body weight during a fall recovery—these are all strength expressions. They require training that challenges the musculature, not placates it.

This cultural framing also explains why many aging adults underestimate how much muscle they've lost. Weight on the scale often remains steady or climbs, giving the illusion of preserved mass. In reality, body composition shifts silently: muscle is replaced by fat, even if total weight doesn't change. This phenomenon, known as sarcopenic obesity, is particularly insidious because it hides the loss behind a stable number. Only when confronted with functional challenges—carrying a suitcase, standing up off the floor, holding balance on one leg—does the extent of decline become obvious. By that point, reversal is harder, though not impossible.

Perhaps the most damaging assumption is that strength training past 50 is a luxury—nice if you have time, irrelevant if you don't. The data paint a very different picture. Muscle is not an aesthetic bonus; it is biological insurance. It is the buffer that stands between an older adult and the hospital bed. It is the mechanism through which blood sugar is controlled, inflammation is modulated, and energy is sustained. Without muscle, the ability to live independently collapses long before life expectancy is reached. You can't medicate your way out of sarcopenia, and cardio won't rescue your quadriceps. The only intervention that halts the free fall is resistance—literal and figurative.

Ultimately, the muscle cliff is not a metaphor. It is a measurable, physiological cascade with real endpoints: falls, fractures, frailty, dependence. The good news—if one can call it that—is that it's not a cliff for those who prepare. With consistent resistance training, muscle mass can be preserved, strength can be regained, and the descent can be transformed into a plateau. But without that intervention, the landing is hard, and the recovery often impossible. Most people don't realize they're falling until they've already hit something.

Chapter 2: Why Cardio Isn't Enough Anymore

For decades, aerobic exercise was marketed as the panacea for aging. Brisk walking, jogging, and cycling earned a reputation as cardiovascular cure-alls—accessible, scalable, and life-extending. While aerobic activity remains beneficial, the physiology of aging demands a recalibration of priorities. After fifty, the body doesn't primarily fail through cardiovascular collapse. It fails through musculoskeletal erosion, insulin resistance, mitochondrial decay, and structural frailty—none of which are adequately addressed by steady-state cardio. The familiar refrain to "just move more" loses precision with age. Not all movement preserves muscle. And not all exercise slows the decline.

Cardio's limitations begin with its insufficient mechanical load. Running may engage muscles, but it rarely overloads them enough to trigger hypertrophy or slow atrophy. Most aerobic activity falls into what's termed the oxidative threshold—intense enough to burn calories and elevate heart rate, but too low in resistance to meaningfully stress muscle fibers, particularly Type II fast-twitch fibers. These are the fibers most responsible for power, balance, and fall prevention, and they're also the first to atrophy with age. Without external resistance, the aging neuromuscular system is under-challenged, leaving strength untapped and motor units idle. Cardio preserves movement capacity, but not necessarily movement competence.

The second issue is metabolic. With aging comes a rising tide of insulin resistance, a process driven in large part by muscle loss. Muscle tissue is the primary site for glucose disposal. The more muscle one has—and uses—the more efficiently blood sugar is cleared. Aerobic exercise does modestly improve glucose uptake during and shortly after training, but resistance training drives long-term improvements in insulin sensitivity by increasing muscle mass and enhancing GLUT-4 transporter activity. In older adults, this becomes critical. A 2017 study in *Diabetologia* showed that progressive resistance training was more effective than aerobic training alone in reversing prediabetes. The implication is clear: a 60-minute walk is good; a loaded squat is better.

Cardio also fails to provide the skeletal stimulus necessary to mitigate osteoporosis. Weight-bearing aerobic activity like walking does exert some ground reaction force, but it pales in comparison to the compressive and tensile loads of resistance training. Bone, like muscle, responds to mechanical stress. Without sufficient load, osteoblast activity declines, and bone density follows. Postmenopausal women, in particular, are vulnerable to bone loss due to estrogen decline. Simply increasing steps per day does not halt this process. In contrast, resistance protocols that include compound lifts—squats, deadlifts, and overhead presses—demonstrate marked improvements in BMD (bone mineral density) over time. A 2015 trial in *Osteoporosis International* found that postmenopausal women engaging in heavy resistance training twice per week saw significant increases in both spine and femoral neck BMD, without increased injury risk. There is no elliptical equivalent to a barbell back squat when it comes to bone preservation.

Cardiovascular training does maintain aerobic capacity, and VO_2 max is indeed a predictor of longevity. But the relevance of VO_2 max must be framed in functional terms. It reflects endurance, not robustness. Most aging-related injuries, hospitalizations, and dependencies don't arise because someone couldn't walk a 5K. They arise because they couldn't rise from the floor. Cardiovascular endurance without muscular strength is like having a full gas tank in a car with no brakes or steering. It may keep you moving, but not in control. Studies tracking health outcomes in older adults consistently find that strength—not aerobic fitness—is the better predictor of mortality. Grip strength, leg press power, and even self-reported lifting capacity have stronger correlations with lifespan and independence than traditional cardio measures.

There's also a recovery cost. As bodies age, recovery capacity diminishes. Every form of training carries a physiological toll. Aerobic sessions, particularly long-distance or high-frequency formats, tax the cardiovascular and immune systems more than commonly appreciated. Endurance athletes over 50 often display elevated cortisol levels, suppressed testosterone, and signs of chronic systemic inflammation. This is not an indictment of cardio, but a caution against over-reliance. When the margin for recovery narrows, efficiency matters. Strength training, especially in low-volume, high-intensity formats, offers a superior return on investment for aging bodies by producing maximal adaptation with minimal systemic stress.

Even the supposed mental benefits of cardio—often cited as superior to resistance training—fail to hold under scrutiny. Both modalities increase endorphin release and promote neurogenesis. However, studies comparing resistance training to aerobic activity in older adults find comparable, and sometimes greater, improvements in mood, cognitive function, and anxiety reduction with lifting. One 2018 meta-analysis in *Sports Medicine* found resistance training significantly reduced depressive symptoms across all age groups, with notable efficacy in older populations. The act of overcoming load—not just accumulating steps—appears to have unique psychological benefits, fostering agency, confidence, and resilience.

The persistence of cardio dominance in public health narratives owes more to inertia than evidence. Walking campaigns and aerobics classes are easier to promote, scale, and commodify. They require no equipment, no instruction, and no confrontation with the intimidating world of weights. But ease does not equate to efficacy. The absence of strength training from older adults' routines isn't just a missed opportunity—it's a failure of prescription. Most general practitioners still default to recommending walking or light aerobic activity because they lack formal education in resistance protocols. The result is a clinical blind spot where muscle continues to vanish under the guise of "staying active."

This is not to dismiss cardio's value. Aerobic training improves circulation, enhances mitochondrial efficiency, and can support cardiovascular health when intelligently programmed. It should remain part of an aging adult's training toolkit. But its utility must be contextualized. Cardio can support aging. It cannot anchor it. Once muscle mass begins its post-50 decline, strength training ceases to be optional. It becomes triage. A 70-year-old with a strong deadlift and adequate lean mass will navigate daily life, metabolic stress, and physical injury far more effectively than one who logs daily walks but can't control their descent onto a toilet seat.

The cultural tendency to place aerobic activity on a pedestal stems from a conflation of effort with outcome. Cardio feels strenuous, it induces sweat, and it signals movement. But aging isn't about feeling tired—it's about resisting entropy. Muscle is the tissue of resistance. Cardio builds endurance; lifting builds capacity. Without capacity, endurance is moot. It's not that cardio becomes harmful with age—it's that it becomes insufficient. And when insufficiency goes uncorrected, decline accelerates.

The final irony is that many of the goals older adults seek through cardio—weight management, vitality, reduced disease risk—are better achieved through muscle. Muscle burns more calories at rest. It improves insulin function, modulates inflammation, and preserves hormonal balance. Yet most over-50 training programs prescribe cardio like a default medication and treat strength as a niche supplement. This inversion fails biology. The aging body does not need to be reminded how to move—it needs to be re-equipped to handle movement. Cardio sustains movement; strength training sustains the mover.

In sum, cardio isn't the enemy. It simply can't shoulder the burden of aging alone. For those over fifty, longevity isn't built through marathons but through resistance. Not resistance to aging—that's inevitable—but resistance through training, which remains profoundly responsive, even as the decades pile on.

Chapter 3: Strength Is the Real Vital Sign

Blood pressure, cholesterol, and resting heart rate still dominate the conversation when physicians talk about health metrics. But none of them can predict, with consistent accuracy, whether someone will live independently into their 80s—or even survive the next five years. Strength, however, can. It is the only biomarker that directly reflects functional capacity, predicts all-cause mortality, and integrates the performance of multiple systems—neuromuscular, metabolic, skeletal—in one measurable expression. Unlike isolated lab values, strength doesn't lie. It cannot be masked by pharmaceuticals or manipulated by fasting before a blood test. It reflects what a body can actually do, not what it looks like on paper.

Among the most consistent findings in gerontology research is the link between grip strength and survival. A 2015 Lancet study spanning 17 countries found that every 5-kilogram decrease in grip strength correlated with a 16% increase in all-cause mortality. This was independent of age, sex, smoking, and comorbidities. Grip strength, though seemingly banal, acts as a proxy for total body strength and overall neuromuscular integrity. It correlates not just with muscle mass but with coordination, reaction time, and even cognitive health. The hand's ability to exert force is a downstream reflection of central nervous system efficiency, tendon integrity, and muscular health across the entire upper kinetic chain. Yet it rarely enters the diagnostic toolkit outside of specialized settings.

More dramatically, lower body strength—particularly in the legs—is even more predictive of future autonomy. A 2022 study in *The Journals of Gerontology* examined leg press strength in adults over 60 and found that those in the lowest quartile were four times more likely to experience disability within five years. Stair ascent time, chair rise ability, and gait speed all derive primarily from quadriceps and gluteal function. These are not trivial benchmarks. Slower gait speed alone is associated with higher hospitalization rates, cognitive decline, and early death. Unlike cardiovascular endurance, which can be preserved to some degree by walking, lower-body strength requires intentional, loaded movement. There is no casual substitute for squatting against resistance.

The problem with conventional vital signs is that they track risk, not readiness. Blood pressure may indicate arterial strain, and cholesterol may signal plaque buildup, but neither tells you whether someone can get up from the floor unaided, carry groceries up stairs, or brace against a fall. Strength, in contrast, is the real-time readiness metric. It reflects whether the body's systems are primed to respond, recover, and adapt. This readiness is not academic. It determines whether an older adult returns home after surgery or enters long-term care. The presence or absence of strength is the difference between resilience and fragility.

Sarcopenia is the silent siphon of this resilience, and its early detection depends on identifying strength decline—not weight loss, not subjective fatigue. Many older adults appear metabolically stable on lab reports while losing 1–2% of their muscle mass annually. The body compensates until it can't. Then, seemingly out of nowhere, a hospital admission, a fall, or a pneumonia diagnosis reveals the extent of the deficit. Those who enter acute medical care in a weakened state exit weaker still. In-hospital muscle loss can exceed 1 kilogram per week, particularly in patients over 65. Without prior strength reserves, recovery stalls. The absence of muscular reserve is not just a health inconvenience—it is a mortality risk.

The healthcare system's reluctance to include strength as a vital sign is not grounded in science but in logistics. Measuring strength requires time, equipment, and some form of physical engagement, none of which fit neatly into a 12-minute clinical appointment. By contrast, blood pressure cuffs and lab panels are passive, quick, and reimbursable. But this convenience creates a blind spot. A person may pass every conventional screening and still be one slip away from a fractured hip and permanent dependency. Strength testing—grip dynamometry, sit-to-stand assessments, deadlift capability—requires presence and participation. It demands that the patient do something, not just be examined. For an aging population, this difference is critical.

Strength also reveals more than physical capacity. It indexes how the nervous system, muscular system, and connective tissues coordinate under tension. In resistance training, the ability to progressively overload the system reflects adaptability. If someone can lift 10% more than they could six weeks ago, their physiology has not just maintained—it has improved. No standard vital sign can capture that. You cannot quantify adaptation by resting heart rate alone. But strength is dynamic. It evolves in real time with training. It can be built, lost, and rebuilt, all while reflecting underlying biological resilience.

Even in terminal illness, strength remains predictive. Oncology literature increasingly recognizes muscle mass and strength as determinants of chemotherapy tolerance and survival. A 2019 study in *Cancer Medicine* found that patients with higher strength scores—measured by handgrip—had significantly lower treatment toxicity and longer survival, even when cancer staging was equivalent. This principle extends beyond cancer. In chronic obstructive pulmonary disease, heart failure, and renal disease, muscular strength often outpaces organ-specific measures in predicting outcomes. The body, it turns out, does not deteriorate in isolated systems. It declines as an integrated whole—and strength measures that integration better than any lab value.

Resistance training, then, is not just exercise—it is a diagnostic tool and a form of therapy. A set of well-executed squats reveals gluteal power, core stability, spinal integrity, and ankle mobility all at once. A proper deadlift recruits posterior chain coordination, grip strength, and hip extension force. These are more than lifts; they are assessments. Each repetition is both a treatment and a test. For aging adults, the barbell is not an athletic implement—it is a diagnostic platform. It answers questions no stethoscope can.

Despite all this, strength is rarely discussed as essential unless performance is the goal. Even among active older adults, cardiovascular conditioning is prioritized, and strength relegated to "supplemental" work. This hierarchy persists even as data continues to show that strength, not cardio endurance, is what predicts whether a person can age independently. The reason is partly historical. Aerobic exercise became synonymous with heart health during the 1970s public health campaigns, and its dominance in clinical recommendations has gone largely unchallenged. But what protects against sudden cardiac death at 50 is not what sustains functional life at 80. At some point, maintaining circulation ceases to be the priority. Maintaining sovereignty over one's body becomes the only goal that matters.

No one is arguing against the relevance of cardiovascular fitness. But when an 82-year-old cannot get up from the floor, the issue is not a lack of aerobic capacity. It's strength. When a 70-year-old struggles with grocery bags, the heart isn't the limiter—the muscles are. Function degrades not from disease in isolation, but from the loss of power to resist gravity. It's not pressure in the arteries, but torque at the joints. These realities do not show up in blood panels. They show up in parking lots, stairwells, and bathroom floors.

Reframing strength as a vital sign demands a shift not just in medical assessment but in personal priorities. The question is no longer "What's your blood pressure?" but "How much weight can you safely lift today compared to six months ago?" That question cannot be faked. It forces direct engagement with the truth of the body. And while the answer may be humbling, it is also actionable. Strength can be measured. It can be improved. It can be preserved. And once it becomes the standard against which aging is assessed, everything else— mobility, metabolism, longevity—starts to make a lot more sense.

Chapter 4: Mitochondria: The Energy Crisis in Aging Muscles

By the sixth decade of life, energy decline is nearly universal, but its true origin is rarely acknowledged. Fatigue, once dismissed as a normal part of aging, is now better understood as a byproduct of cellular dysfunction—specifically mitochondrial decay. These microscopic powerhouses, responsible for generating the bulk of cellular ATP, do not merely weaken with age; they downregulate, fragment, and lose efficiency in ways that fundamentally impair muscular performance and systemic vitality. Nowhere is this more evident than in skeletal muscle, where mitochondrial dysfunction contributes directly to sarcopenia, insulin resistance, and physical frailty. The paradox is that while aging reduces mitochondrial capacity, it also increases the need for mitochondrial resilience. And there is only one intervention shown to consistently reverse this trajectory: resistance training.

In older muscle tissue, mitochondria exhibit both structural and functional deterioration. Electron microscopy reveals swollen, disorganized organelles with diminished cristae surface area—the internal folds essential for ATP synthesis. Functionally, this translates to decreased oxidative phosphorylation, meaning less usable energy is produced per unit of substrate. The result is a cellular economy in crisis. Tasks that were once metabolically inexpensive—climbing stairs, standing from a chair, walking uphill—suddenly require disproportionate effort. Compounding this, reactive oxygen species (ROS) production rises with mitochondrial inefficiency, leading to oxidative damage of DNA, lipids, and proteins. This oxidative stress accelerates cellular aging and triggers apoptotic pathways, which contribute to muscle fiber loss, particularly of the fast-twitch variety. Fatigue, then, is not a vague symptom; it is a downstream effect of mitochondrial failure.

Importantly, aerobic exercise does offer some mitochondrial benefit, but its effects plateau in older adults without sufficient muscular tension. Mitochondrial biogenesis—the process by which new mitochondria are formed—is primarily stimulated by PGC-1α, a coactivator upregulated by both endurance and resistance exercise. Yet studies consistently show that resistance training, especially when performed at high intensity, evokes greater mitochondrial remodeling in aging muscle. A landmark 2007 trial published in *PLOS One* demonstrated that six months of progressive resistance training in adults over 65 reversed age-related gene expression in mitochondrial pathways by nearly 600 genes, restoring youthful metabolic profiles in muscle biopsies. No pharmaceutical intervention has come close to producing such systemic reversal.

Mechanically, resistance training triggers mitochondrial adaptation through repeated cycles of high-tension muscular contraction and recovery. These contractions increase calcium flux, mechanical stress, and metabolic demand—conditions that signal the need for greater mitochondrial capacity. As the muscle adapts to lifting heavier loads, it does so not just by enlarging fibers but by upgrading their metabolic infrastructure. More mitochondria are built. Existing ones become more efficient. Enzymes involved in oxidative metabolism are upregulated. These changes translate to more efficient ATP production, improved endurance under load, and lower baseline fatigue. Muscle stops behaving like a decaying engine and starts running like a modern hybrid—powerful, efficient, and resilient.

The location of this mitochondrial restoration is also significant. Unlike endurance training, which preferentially improves mitochondria in Type I fibers, resistance training stimulates adaptations in Type II fibers—the very fibers most vulnerable to age-related atrophy. These fast-twitch units are responsible for rapid force production, fall recovery, and power output. Their mitochondrial density is typically lower, but their function is essential to everyday tasks like rising quickly from a seated position or catching oneself during a misstep. Resistance training forces these fibers to stay online. Without it, they wither, and the energetic cost of movement becomes exponentially greater.

The systemic implications of mitochondrial decline extend far beyond the muscles themselves. Poor mitochondrial function in skeletal muscle is linked to insulin resistance, as impaired oxidative metabolism disrupts glucose uptake and utilization. It also contributes to chronic inflammation via activation of the NLRP3 inflammasome, a key mediator in age-related degenerative diseases. Resistance training disrupts this inflammatory feedback loop by improving mitochondrial health and reducing excess ROS production. This is not anecdotal. A 2019 study in *Cell Metabolism* found that older adults who engaged in 12 weeks of resistance training showed marked reductions in circulating inflammatory cytokines, concurrent with increased mitochondrial enzyme activity in muscle biopsies. Lifting weights, in this context, is not merely a muscular intervention—it is a systemic metabolic therapy.

There is also a neurological dimension to this restoration. Mitochondria in muscle tissue influence not just local energy supply but also neural efficiency. Aging muscles experience denervation, in which motor units lose connection with their corresponding nerves. Resistance training, by stimulating both the muscle and its neural inputs, slows this process. The resulting neuromuscular signaling maintains coordination, proprioception, and reflexive balance. These effects are not theoretical. Older adults who engage in regular strength training demonstrate faster nerve conduction velocities and more stable motor unit firing patterns. At the mitochondrial level, this is supported by reduced oxidative stress in peripheral nerves, preserving their ability to transmit signals effectively. In essence, lifting keeps both the wires and the batteries functional.

One of the most counterintuitive findings in this domain is that the energy crisis of aging cannot be solved by rest. Rest conserves what energy remains but does not address the reason energy is diminishing. Only the stimulus of muscular challenge—progressive overload, high-tension contraction— activates the cellular machinery needed to generate more capacity. This principle is frequently misunderstood, leading many older adults to cut back on effort when they feel tired, rather than recognizing that fatigue often signals undertrained, not overused, tissue. In this sense, low energy is not a barrier to resistance training; it is a reason for it.

The prevailing myth that older adults should avoid intense resistance training out of caution is not only baseless—it's counterproductive. Mitochondrial decline accelerates in the absence of load. Age-associated declines in VO_2 max and metabolic flexibility are not just consequences of time but of inaction. By the time fatigue becomes chronic, the cellular underpinnings are already entrenched. Reversing them takes work. But the muscle remains remarkably plastic. Mitochondria respond to challenge at any age. Studies involving individuals in their 80s and even 90s have documented robust mitochondrial improvements following structured resistance protocols. These aren't isolated cases of athletic anomalies—they are normal human responses to a stimulus that was absent for too long.

None of this implies that resistance training alone is sufficient for every mitochondrial parameter. Nutrition, sleep, and micronutrient status all play supporting roles. However, without the mechanical stimulus of resistance, no combination of supplements or aerobic activity can regenerate mitochondrial density or restore oxidative efficiency in Type II muscle fibers. Pills may support the system, but only training rewires it.

Ultimately, the decline in mitochondrial function is not a mystery. It is a predictable consequence of reduced muscular demand. The fix is equally clear: increase demand, progressively and persistently, through resistance. While the modern aging narrative still frames fatigue as an inevitability, the biological evidence tells another story. Muscles are tired not because they are old, but because they are untrained. And energy is not something you save—it's something you earn.

Chapter 5: Insulin Resistance Starts in the Quads

Insulin resistance is often framed as a dietary issue, a product of sugar overconsumption and poor metabolic choices. While nutrition undoubtedly plays a role, the more primary culprit sits beneath the surface: loss of skeletal muscle. Specifically, the decline in large muscle groups like the quadriceps—the major movers of the lower body—initiates a cascade that impairs glucose disposal long before blood sugar ever appears elevated on a lab report. Insulin resistance, in this context, is not merely a result of what's eaten but a reflection of what's missing. And what's missing is contractile tissue capable of handling metabolic load.

Skeletal muscle is the body's largest site of glucose uptake. After a carbohydrate-rich meal, insulin drives glucose into muscle cells via GLUT-4 transporters. These transporters are activated both by insulin itself and by muscle contraction. In healthy muscle, this two-pronged system operates efficiently: insulin rises, GLUT-4 moves to the cell membrane, and glucose enters the cell to be oxidized or stored as glycogen. But with aging and inactivity, two simultaneous degradations occur. First, the sheer volume of muscle declines, meaning there are fewer total GLUT-4 receptors available. Second, the insulin signaling pathway becomes blunted, reducing the muscle's responsiveness. The end result is excess glucose circulating longer in the bloodstream, prompting the pancreas to release more insulin to compensate. Over time, this compensation becomes maladaptive. Cells stop listening. The system collapses into chronic hyperinsulinemia and, eventually, type 2 diabetes.

The quadriceps, glutes, and hamstrings are the largest muscle groups in the body, and they are also the most insulin-sensitive when trained. Their sheer mass means they act as glucose sponges—capable of clearing significant blood sugar loads after meals. When these muscles are maintained or hypertrophied through resistance training, they provide an enormous metabolic buffer. But when they atrophy, especially post-50, the capacity for glucose disposal contracts dramatically. This is why many people who appear metabolically healthy for decades suddenly develop impaired fasting glucose in their late fifties or sixties, despite unchanged diets. The infrastructure needed to handle glucose has quietly disappeared.

This also explains why weight loss alone often fails to resolve insulin resistance in older adults. A person can lose fat and still be metabolically dysfunctional if they've also lost muscle mass. Indeed, intentional weight loss without resistance training often worsens insulin sensitivity by further reducing lean mass. A 2011 study in *The New England Journal of Medicine* compared different interventions in obese adults with type 2 diabetes and found that combining resistance training with moderate caloric restriction was more effective in improving insulin sensitivity than diet alone. It's not just about shrinking fat cells; it's about restoring muscle cells.

Crucially, the mechanism of improvement goes beyond mass. Resistance training enhances muscle cell insulin sensitivity even without hypertrophy. One of the key adaptations involves increased mitochondrial density and improved oxidative capacity, which enhances the muscle's ability to oxidize glucose. In addition, training increases the expression and translocation efficiency of GLUT-4 receptors, meaning that even existing muscle becomes more efficient at glucose uptake. A 2013 study in *Diabetes Care* demonstrated that as little as 12 weeks of progressive resistance training improved insulin action in older adults with prediabetes, independent of weight loss. The intervention did not merely reduce blood sugar—it altered the metabolic behavior of the tissue responsible for regulating it.

It's worth noting that aerobic training also improves insulin sensitivity, but the effect is less durable and more dependent on frequency. Miss a few cardio sessions, and the benefit dissipates rapidly. In contrast, resistance training yields longer-lasting effects due to the structural changes it imposes on the musculature and associated metabolic machinery. Muscle gained or strengthened through resistance doesn't just help during exercise—it improves glucose handling at rest, throughout the day, during sleep, and in response to meals. Its effects are chronic, not just acute.

The implications are staggering when viewed in terms of public health. Nearly one in three American adults over 60 meets criteria for prediabetes. The standard medical response involves dietary modification and, increasingly, pharmaceutical intervention—metformin, GLP-1 agonists, and other insulin-sensitizing drugs. These may blunt hyperglycemia, but they do not restore lost muscle or improve muscle-specific glucose handling. They treat symptoms while ignoring the core dysfunction. No pill can replace the metabolic role of the quadriceps. Yet few physicians recommend progressive strength training as a first-line therapy. This is not an oversight—it's a knowledge gap. Most medical curricula devote minimal attention to skeletal muscle as a metabolic organ. As a result, patients are told to "eat less sugar" rather than "squat more often."

What's often overlooked is the bidirectional relationship between muscle and insulin sensitivity. Not only does muscle improve glucose uptake—it also responds to improved insulin signaling by growing more efficiently. When insulin sensitivity is restored, protein synthesis pathways become more responsive to resistance training. In other words, improving insulin function through training makes future training more effective, creating a feedback loop of metabolic and structural enhancement. Conversely, when insulin resistance is present, anabolic signaling becomes blunted, reducing muscle growth and compounding sarcopenia. The longer resistance is delayed, the steeper the metabolic hill becomes.

This dynamic is especially critical for postmenopausal women, who experience both estrogen decline and accelerated muscle loss. Estrogen plays a supportive role in glucose metabolism, and its reduction amplifies insulin resistance risk. Resistance training can mitigate both effects—improving muscle mass while restoring some of the glucose tolerance lost through hormonal shifts. A 2014 study in *Menopause* showed that resistance training in postmenopausal women led to significant improvements in HOMA-IR scores, a marker of insulin resistance, even in the absence of significant fat loss. For these women, the answer is not more restriction—it's more force production.

The term "metabolic health" remains vague in mainstream usage, often reduced to fasting glucose and body mass index.

But true metabolic health depends on dynamic tissue function—how much glucose a muscle can clear, how fast it can respond to insulin, how resilient it remains under daily metabolic demand. These are not passive traits. They require training, and that training must be specific. Walking or light cardio may preserve general mobility, but it will not sufficiently activate or grow the muscle fibers most responsible for metabolic regulation. The quadriceps do not become insulin sensitive from casual use. They require load, progression, and mechanical stress.

In aging adults, this becomes a matter of metabolic survival. Once muscle loss crosses a threshold, even small dietary indiscretions provoke exaggerated glucose excursions. Post-meal fatigue, sugar cravings, and unexplained weight gain aren't failures of discipline—they're signals of muscular deficiency. Food is not being poorly chosen; it's being poorly handled. And the handler is the muscle, or what remains of it. By restoring strength, especially in the lower body, the metabolic machinery needed to process food efficiently can be rebuilt.

Insulin resistance doesn't start in the pancreas or the liver. It starts in the quads, where glucose was supposed to go but no longer can. Reversing this isn't a matter of dieting harder—it's a matter of lifting smarter.

Chapter 6: Hormonal Armor: Testosterone, Estrogen, and Muscle

After fifty, the hormonal landscape begins to shift in ways that compromise strength, energy, and resilience. Testosterone in men and estrogen in women don't vanish overnight, but their gradual decline reshapes the body's ability to maintain lean mass, repair tissue, regulate metabolism, and sustain libido and cognition. These aren't superficial losses—they are central to aging itself. And while hormone replacement therapies dominate the medical response, they overlook a critical fact: muscle mass doesn't just depend on hormones; it helps regulate them. Resistance training doesn't merely offset hormonal decline—it directly intervenes in the feedback loop that determines how these hormones function. In aging bodies, muscle isn't just a recipient of hormonal support—it becomes an active modulator.

Testosterone declines at roughly one percent per year in men after age thirty. But the rate and impact of that decline are profoundly influenced by physical activity. Inactive men lose more testosterone, more quickly. Sarcopenia accelerates, visceral fat accumulates, and metabolic function begins to deteriorate. Resistance training halts much of this. It triggers acute spikes in testosterone post-exercise, increases muscle-specific androgen receptor density, and reduces the inflammatory conditions that suppress hormone production. A 2012 study in *The Journal of Strength and Conditioning Research* showed that older men who followed a structured lifting protocol three times per week significantly improved free testosterone levels and enhanced androgen sensitivity in their muscle tissue. The benefit wasn't purely hormonal—it was functional. The tissue became more responsive to what testosterone remained.

In women, the loss of estrogen after menopause is sharper and biologically more destabilizing. Estrogen supports muscle repair, bone integrity, mitochondrial function, and insulin sensitivity. As levels decline, muscle wasting accelerates, and fat gain, especially in the abdominal region, becomes more pronounced. The usual response is to recommend hormone therapy, yet resistance training proves more effective at maintaining muscle and metabolic function even in estrogen-depleted bodies. A 2015 study in *Menopause* demonstrated that postmenopausal women who engaged in twice-weekly strength training increased lean mass, improved insulin sensitivity, and reduced visceral fat—without any pharmacological intervention. The body, when trained, remains metabolically capable, even in the absence of hormonal abundance.

What resistance training offers is not a reversal of aging, but a recalibration of how the hormonal system operates under strain. With age, not only do hormone levels drop, but tissues become less responsive to them. This is where strength training alters the terrain. It doesn't just stimulate hormone production; it makes the body more efficient at using what's available. Androgen and estrogen receptor expression increases in trained muscle, allowing smaller hormonal signals to produce greater physiological effect. A 2018 study in *The Journal of Applied Physiology* confirmed that older adults who lifted regularly maintained higher receptor density in skeletal muscle, effectively amplifying hormonal utility despite lower circulating levels.

The effect doesn't stop with testosterone and estrogen. Growth hormone (GH) and insulin-like growth factor 1 (IGF-1)—key drivers of tissue regeneration and recovery—also decline with age, contributing to longer recovery times and reduced muscle-building capacity. Yet resistance training, particularly at moderate to high intensities, increases GH secretion and upregulates IGF-1 activity in muscle cells. This isn't anecdotal. A 2014 paper in *Experimental Gerontology* found that older adults who trained consistently had higher post-exercise GH levels and greater IGF-1 sensitivity, leading to better repair, better performance, and better retention of lean mass. These aren't peripheral hormones; they are the body's repair crew. Lifting calls them back into action.

Meanwhile, strength training directly reduces the hormonal interference caused by adipose tissue. Fat is not inert. Visceral fat in particular acts as an endocrine disruptor—converting testosterone into estrogen in men, and contributing to estrogen dominance and insulin resistance in women. By increasing lean mass and reducing visceral fat, resistance training improves the hormonal signal-to-noise ratio. It doesn't just alter levels—it reduces distortion. Cortisol, the catabolic hormone elevated by stress and associated with muscle breakdown, also declines in response to consistent lifting. A 2020 review in *Psychoneuroendocrinology* concluded that strength training led to significant reductions in baseline cortisol among older adults, thereby reducing one of the primary hormonal drivers of age-related muscle loss.

These aren't small effects, and they aren't cosmetic. Hormonal health in later life is tightly correlated with autonomy, resilience, and disease resistance. Low testosterone and low estrogen are both linked to higher mortality, faster cognitive decline, and increased risk of metabolic syndrome. While pharmaceutical interventions can raise blood levels, they cannot fix receptor sensitivity or reverse the tissue degradation that reduces hormonal impact. Muscle, when trained, does both. It is not a passive object requiring hormonal maintenance—it is a regulatory system in its own right.

The cultural narrative around hormones tends to separate them from behavior. Testosterone is often treated as a chemical destiny for men—rising and falling without much influence. Estrogen is seen as something to be replaced or endured. This narrative misses the physiological reality. Hormones do not act in isolation. Their function is mediated by the tissues they target, and those tissues—especially muscle—are modifiable. Resistance training doesn't simply react to hormonal status. It changes it.

This has implications for how medical systems approach aging. Hormone panels are ordered, prescriptions written, and yet muscle mass rarely enters the conversation. Few clinicians ask whether the patient is squatting, pressing, or deadlifting. Yet those movements do more to improve hormonal function than any pill or patch. Hormone replacement therapy may be necessary in some cases, but its effectiveness is heavily dependent on the muscular context in which it operates. You can't inject your way out of frailty. You have to train your way out of it.

That reality should inform how aging individuals prioritize their health interventions. Instead of pursuing hormonal optimization through supplementation alone, they should pursue muscular responsiveness through strength. Lifting won't restore hormones to youthful levels, but it will maximize what remains and repair the machinery that interprets those signals. That includes receptor density, neuromuscular activation, and downstream metabolic behavior. It isn't a workaround for aging—it's the primary defense.

In both men and women, then, muscle becomes the structure through which hormones continue to matter. It converts declining signals into preserved function. It allows a 60-year-old to recover from training, a 70-year-old to retain libido, an 80-year-old to rise unaided from the floor. These are hormonal effects—but they're mediated by load. Resistance training keeps the body listening to the signals it still has. And once muscle stops responding, hormones lose their influence.

Aging without strength training means surrendering hormonal control to entropy. Aging with strength training means preserving, and in some cases restoring, the capacity to adapt. Hormones don't vanish—they stop being used. The fix is simple, if not easy. Train the muscle, and the system stays online. Fail to train it, and even the best hormone panel won't save you.

Chapter 7: Fall Prevention Is a Strength Issue

Falls in older adults are often mischaracterized as coordination mishaps or balance failures, as though the body simply forgets where the floor is. But behind every misplaced step or slow reaction is a deeper truth: the strength wasn't there to correct the movement. Fall prevention is not a matter of practicing careful walking or attending balance classes that shuffle around on foam pads—it is a matter of building the muscular strength and power necessary to recover from instability. Weakness, not clumsiness, is the root cause of most falls past fifty. And unless it is reversed with load-bearing strength training, no amount of mindful movement will prevent the eventual collapse.

The data is unequivocal. One in four adults over 65 falls each year, and falls are the leading cause of injury-related death in this age group. But the precipitating factors are rarely as sudden as they appear. Loss of balance is not a discrete event—it is the outcome of declining force production, particularly in the lower body. As quadriceps strength fades, reaction time slows. As gluteal function erodes, gait becomes unstable. As core control weakens, posture deteriorates. These muscular deficits compound subtly, until one awkward step or minor obstacle reveals just how incapable the body has become of catching itself. The fall is only the visible symptom. The cause has been accumulating for years.

The notion that balance can be trained in isolation—by standing on one foot or walking heel-to-toe—is deeply flawed. Balance is not a skill separate from strength; it is a byproduct of it. What appears to be poor balance is usually poor force output. The body detects perturbation—a shift in weight, an uneven surface—and sends a motor command to adjust. If the muscles cannot generate enough torque quickly enough, correction fails. Strength, particularly rate of force development, is what allows the body to respond to instability with speed and power. Without it, the system behaves like a car with worn brakes and delayed steering. You can stay on the road—until something unexpected happens.

A 2013 meta-analysis in *British Medical Journal* found that resistance training was significantly more effective at reducing fall risk in older adults than either balance training or flexibility programs. The most protective interventions were those that increased lower-body strength and explosive capacity, particularly in the hip extensors and knee stabilizers. This makes intuitive sense. These are the muscle groups responsible for rapid postural correction, lateral stepping, and vertical bracing—all critical during a stumble or misstep. In contrast, balance drills that lack external load may improve proprioception slightly, but they do not increase the contractile strength needed to recover from destabilization under real-world conditions.

Further evidence comes from trials involving power training in older adults. Unlike traditional resistance training focused on slow, controlled reps, power training emphasizes speed of contraction under moderate load. This style of training improves the rate at which muscles can develop force—a key determinant in fall recovery, where milliseconds separate correction from collapse. A 2015 study in *The Journals of Gerontology* showed that older adults who performed explosive resistance movements—such as rapid leg presses and jump squats with light weights—had superior outcomes in dynamic balance and fewer falls over a 12-month follow-up compared to those performing slow-tempo strength training alone. In aging, it's not just how much strength you have; it's how fast you can use it.

Equally important is the role of eccentric strength—the ability to control movement while lengthening muscles. During a fall, it's often eccentric control that determines whether a person can decelerate themselves or crashes to the ground. For example, descending stairs requires strong eccentric contraction of the quadriceps and glutes. Weakness here doesn't just lead to stumbling—it leads to catastrophic unloading, where the legs buckle rather than brake. Resistance training, particularly through movements like controlled step-downs and Romanian deadlifts, trains this deceleration capacity. It teaches the body not just to produce force, but to absorb it safely.

The obsession with flexibility as a primary mode of fall prevention also misleads. While joint mobility is important, it contributes very little without the strength to stabilize within that range. Loose hamstrings do not prevent falls; strong glutes do. The person who can deadlift their bodyweight from the floor has a far greater margin of error than someone who can touch their toes but can't get up unassisted from a chair. True mobility—functional range of motion under tension—requires strength at every point along the movement arc. And only resistance training builds that capacity.

This also reframes the role of footwear, assistive devices, and home safety modifications. These are useful, even necessary, in some cases. But they are not solutions—they are crutches for a problem that training can address more directly. A grab bar by the toilet compensates for insufficient hip and thigh strength. A walker supports a body that has lost the ability to stand without assistance. These tools have their place, but their growing ubiquity reflects a culture resigned to physical decline rather than committed to reversing it. A body trained under load does not need a handrail to sit down—it generates its own support.

There is also a psychological dimension to fall risk that strength training addresses uniquely. Fear of falling is one of the strongest predictors of actual falls, creating a feedback loop where anxiety leads to reduced movement, which leads to deconditioning, which further increases the likelihood of a fall. Resistance training breaks this loop by restoring confidence through demonstrated capability. When older adults learn to hinge, squat, lunge, and press under controlled load, they are not just strengthening muscles—they are reshaping their sense of agency. The ability to control one's own body under tension translates into real-world confidence, reducing hesitation and improving movement quality across daily tasks.

Hospital data supports the functional outcomes of strength training in fall prevention. Among adults over 70 admitted for fall-related injuries, the majority show measurable weakness in lower body strength and grip power. Post-discharge rehabilitation rarely includes meaningful resistance training, relying instead on mobility exercises and supervised walking. As a result, many patients never regain full independence. The second fall often comes within a year. And with each successive incident, the odds of full recovery diminish. This cycle is not an inevitability—it is a failure to address the primary variable: inadequate strength.

The strongest defense against this spiral is to build a body that can resist sudden demands. Fall prevention is not reactive—it's proactive. It begins with loading the tissues responsible for movement control and stability before an accident occurs. Strength is not insurance; it is armor. It reduces not only the risk of falling but the severity of consequences if a fall does occur. A person with strong bones, dense muscle, and high power output will hit the ground less often—and recover better when they do.

The message is not complicated. If you want to prevent falls, strengthen the legs, train the hips, load the spine, and challenge the nervous system to respond under pressure. Wobble boards and yoga mats have their place, but they do not substitute for a barbell. Fall risk does not emerge from nowhere—it emerges from the slow, steady erosion of strength. Rebuilding that strength is not theoretical. It's practical, measurable, and within reach—at any age.

Chapter 8: Bone Density and Lifting Iron

Osteoporosis is often portrayed as a silent thief, quietly stealing density from bones until one day a hip fractures from a routine fall or a vertebra compresses under the weight of standing up. But this metaphor obscures what is actually a highly predictable, highly preventable biological event: bones weaken because they are not loaded. After age 50, this process accelerates, particularly in postmenopausal women, but it is neither mysterious nor inevitable. The human skeleton, much like muscle, adapts to the demands placed upon it. And when those demands vanish, bones deteriorate—first in mass, then in structure, and eventually in function. The only intervention that consistently halts or reverses this trajectory is resistance training. Not pills, not calcium supplements, not low-impact exercise. Iron, lifted and moved against gravity, is the corrective force.

Bone is living tissue. It remodels itself constantly through a balance of osteoblast (building) and osteoclast (breaking down) activity. This process is regulated not just by hormones and nutrients, but by mechanical stress. Specifically, bones respond to strain—compressive, tensile, and torsional forces that stimulate osteocytes to signal for new growth. Walking generates some of this force, but not enough to offset age-related loss. Running offers more, but is often unsustainable or inadvisable for aging joints. The mechanical loading that produces the highest osteogenic response comes from resistance training—movements that load the axial skeleton under significant tension, particularly through compound lifts like squats, deadlifts, overhead presses, and weighted carries.

The superiority of resistance training for bone health is not theoretical. A landmark 2015 study in *Osteoporosis International* examined postmenopausal women performing high-intensity resistance training twice per week for eight months. The protocol included heavy squats, deadlifts, and overhead presses at 80–85% of one-rep max. Participants experienced significant increases in bone mineral density (BMD) at the lumbar spine and femoral neck—precisely the areas most vulnerable to osteoporotic fracture. Notably, there were no injuries. This study dismantled the prevailing assumption that lifting heavy is unsafe for aging women. In reality, not lifting is far more dangerous.

The site-specific nature of bone adaptation is another reason why resistance training outperforms generalized activity. Bones strengthen at the points where strain is applied. Wrist fractures, for example, are common in older adults because few activities place meaningful load on the distal radius. But a properly loaded overhead press, farmer's carry, or push-up variation sends stress directly through the wrists and forearms. Similarly, the vertebrae—another frequent site of age-related fracture—respond to axial compression, which occurs when loading the spine under a bar or carrying weight vertically. Without these signals, bone turnover continues unopposed in the wrong direction. Supplements cannot fix that. Gravity can.

Pharmaceutical interventions for osteoporosis, such as bisphosphonates, do reduce fracture risk by slowing bone resorption. But they do not stimulate new bone growth. Nor do they improve the strength, coordination, or muscle mass necessary to prevent the falls that cause fractures in the first place. These drugs are protective only insofar as they reduce further loss. Resistance training, in contrast, builds. It strengthens the bones and the muscles around them, improving both structural integrity and the capacity to move well enough to avoid impact altogether. The best way to survive a fall is not to fall. The second-best is to hit the ground with bones that can handle it.

This integrative benefit—muscle and bone strengthening simultaneously—is critical. The aging body does not deteriorate in compartments. Muscle loss accelerates bone loss, and vice versa. Sarcopenia and osteoporosis are not distinct processes but overlapping manifestations of underloading. When muscle pulls on bone, as it does during resistance training, both tissues adapt in tandem. A 2020 meta-analysis in *Bone* confirmed that increases in lean mass correlate strongly with increases in bone mineral density in older adults engaged in strength training. This is not coincidence—it is mechanical necessity. The skeleton exists to support movement. Remove movement under load, and the skeleton loses its reason to stay strong.

Despite this, most public health messaging on bone health remains trapped in the realm of dietary recommendations. Calcium and vitamin D are emphasized as though they are the primary determinants of bone integrity. While both are necessary cofactors in bone metabolism, neither generates the structural demand that triggers osteogenesis. A 1000-milligram calcium supplement does not make the femoral neck more resilient during a slip on the stairs. A barbell, however, does— if it's lifted consistently, with progressive overload, and with enough intensity to challenge the skeletal system. That distinction—between enabling nutrients and triggering stimulus—is where most prevention efforts fail.

Even well-meaning advice about "weight-bearing exercise" often falls short. The term is used broadly to describe walking, hiking, or bodyweight routines. But true weight-bearing, in the context of osteogenic stimulus, involves external loading that significantly exceeds body weight. A 60-year-old walking at a brisk pace exerts ground forces equivalent to about 1.2 times bodyweight. A loaded back squat at even moderate intensity can exceed three times bodyweight across the hip and spine. That magnitude of force is what generates the internal signaling necessary for bone formation. Anything less may preserve function but does not reverse decline.

There is also the issue of training velocity. While endurance activity tends to be slow and repetitive, resistance training involves rapid force generation, joint stabilization under load, and complex motor coordination—all of which contribute to fall resistance and impact resilience. Training the body to absorb and redirect force through lifting is functionally equivalent to preparing it for the unpredictable demands of daily life. A trip on uneven pavement doesn't resemble a treadmill session—it resembles an unexpected eccentric load on the glutes, quads, and trunk. A body accustomed to lifting weight under tension can meet that demand. One that isn't gets fractured.

Another overlooked benefit is posture correction. Spinal compression fractures and kyphosis often stem from both poor bone density and weak posterior chain musculature. Deadlifts, rows, and carries reinforce spinal extension under load, improving thoracic alignment and reducing the chronic flexion that increases fracture risk. These are not aesthetic benefits— they are orthopedic ones. A rounded spine is not just a posture issue; it's a structural liability under everyday force.

For older adults, this means that lifting isn't an aggressive choice—it's a conservative one. It is the only known intervention that addresses bone health, muscle mass, joint integrity, and fall resilience simultaneously. The risks of not training—structural decay, fragility fractures, hospitalization—are far higher than the controlled stress imposed by proper resistance training. Safety concerns are real, but they are best mitigated by intelligent programming and progression, not by avoidance.

Bone loss is not a passive consequence of aging. It is a predictable response to physical disengagement. The prescription is straightforward: apply load to the skeleton through planned, progressive resistance. Train the spine, hips, and shoulders under tension. Increase the challenge gradually. Maintain the signal. This is not advanced fitness—it is baseline survival. For anyone over fifty, lifting iron isn't about performance. It's about preserving the scaffolding that keeps the body upright, mobile, and out of the emergency room.

Chapter 9: Fat Gain Is Muscle Loss in Disguise

Weight gain after fifty is often treated as a simple equation of calories in versus calories out, blamed on reduced activity, slower metabolism, or less dietary discipline. But the real mechanism operates at a deeper level. What appears to be creeping fat accumulation is often the downstream effect of muscle loss—a silent restructuring of the body's metabolic engine. As skeletal muscle diminishes, the capacity to burn energy at rest drops, insulin sensitivity declines, and the hormonal environment shifts toward fat storage. The scale goes up, the belt tightens, and the assumption is overeating. In reality, the body is metabolically downsizing because its primary energy consumer—muscle—is vanishing.

This process begins gradually but accelerates with age. Skeletal muscle accounts for a significant portion of total daily energy expenditure, even at rest. It is highly metabolically active tissue, requiring constant ATP turnover to maintain protein synthesis, ion transport, and structural integrity. When muscle mass decreases, resting metabolic rate (RMR) drops. Studies estimate that between the ages of 30 and 80, RMR declines by about 25%, and the majority of that decline is directly attributable to muscle loss rather than age alone. In short, the body becomes more efficient at conserving energy because it has less tissue to maintain. This efficiency is not a benefit—it's a signal that the system is adapting to weakness.

This metabolic shift explains why many aging adults gain fat despite maintaining the same diet and physical activity level they had in their 30s or 40s. The caloric intake hasn't changed, but the caloric requirement has. The metabolic infrastructure needed to process and utilize those calories has atrophied. Protein isn't absorbed as effectively, glucose isn't cleared as quickly, and lipids are stored more readily. The fat gain that follows isn't just about excess—it's about mismatch. The body is running a 2000-calorie operating system on what used to be a 2500-calorie machine.

This is compounded by anabolic resistance, the age-related blunting of the body's response to protein intake and mechanical load. Older adults require a higher protein dose and a stronger training stimulus to achieve the same muscle-building response as younger individuals. Without stimulus, muscle degradation outpaces synthesis, and the resulting lean mass deficit reduces not only strength but metabolic flexibility—the ability to shift between fuel sources efficiently. As this flexibility erodes, the body becomes increasingly biased toward fat storage, even during periods of energy balance. The gain in fat mass is not a standalone issue; it is the visible symptom of internal muscle withdrawal.

One of the most deceptive aspects of this process is that it can occur even in those who remain "active." Walking, recreational cycling, or light cardio may preserve some degree of cardiovascular health, but they do little to prevent muscle loss or maintain metabolic rate. These activities lack the mechanical tension and progressive overload required to stimulate hypertrophy. As a result, body composition deteriorates quietly, often without any change in the scale. A person may weigh the same at 65 as they did at 45 but have dramatically higher fat mass and lower lean mass—a condition known as sarcopenic obesity. This body type is at elevated risk for insulin resistance, frailty, and cardiovascular disease, despite appearing "normal weight" on paper.

The solution is not aggressive dieting, which typically exacerbates the problem. Caloric restriction without resistance training accelerates muscle loss. The body, sensing an energy shortage, prioritizes lean tissue catabolism, particularly when dietary protein is inadequate. This explains why so many older adults lose weight but become weaker and softer in the process. The number on the scale goes down, but function deteriorates. Metabolic health worsens, not improves. A 2011 study in *The American Journal of Clinical Nutrition* showed that older adults who lost weight through diet alone lost significantly more muscle and less fat compared to those who combined dieting with resistance training. The prescription is clear: if weight loss is pursued, it must be anchored in strength preservation.

Strength training reverses this trajectory by increasing muscle mass and restoring metabolic demand. With more lean tissue, resting energy expenditure rises, glucose uptake improves, and fat oxidation becomes more efficient. Even without weight loss, body composition improves—a shift that matters far more than scale change. A 2017 study in *Obesity* found that resistance training, independent of caloric restriction, led to reductions in visceral fat and improvements in insulin sensitivity in older adults. This is not an aesthetic upgrade; it is a metabolic repair.

Moreover, lifting changes not just what the body stores, but where it stores it. Muscle acts as a metabolic sink, drawing glucose and fatty acids away from storage depots like the liver and abdomen. As muscle mass increases, ectopic fat—fat stored in organs where it doesn't belong—tends to decrease. This redistribution has a profound impact on disease risk. Central adiposity, not total fat mass, is the real driver of metabolic syndrome and cardiovascular pathology in older adults. Resistance training doesn't just reduce the volume of fat; it alters its location and its biochemical behavior.

Fat gain, in this framework, becomes less a failure of willpower and more a consequence of undertraining. When the muscular system is neglected, the metabolic rate adapts downward, nutrient partitioning worsens, and hormonal signals shift in favor of storage over utilization. Leptin sensitivity declines, ghrelin increases, and appetite regulation becomes erratic. The person eats the same but feels hungrier, stores more, and burns less. Muscle is not just a calorie-burning engine—it is the regulator of hunger, energy use, and storage. When it disappears, the system becomes uncalibrated.

Hormones also play a mediating role in this process. Declining testosterone and estrogen exacerbate fat gain and muscle loss, but their effects are modulated by physical activity. Resistance training improves androgen receptor density and estrogen signaling in muscle tissue, making even low hormone levels more effective. It also improves insulin sensitivity, which governs how nutrients are allocated between fat and muscle. In an untrained state, those nutrients are routed to storage. In a trained state, they are used for repair, growth, and energy. The same meal produces vastly different outcomes depending on what the body is primed to do with it.

The key insight is that fat gain after fifty is not a primary disorder—it is the byproduct of declining muscle mass and strength. The answer, then, is not to fight fat directly but to restore the muscle that prevents its accumulation. Dieting harder, moving more, or tracking every macro may yield some results, but without the structural foundation of muscle, the progress is brittle and temporary. The only lasting change comes from rebuilding the tissue that once kept the system balanced.

In this context, body composition becomes the true diagnostic. Not weight. Not BMI. Not vague advice about moderation. The question is: how much muscle remains, and how functional is it? Because if the muscle is gone, the fat isn't just coming—it's already here. It arrived not because something was added, but because something essential was lost. And getting it back starts with resistance, load, and the willingness to lift more than bodyweight demands.

Chapter 10: You're Not Tired, You're Weak

Fatigue is one of the most common complaints after fifty. It's described vaguely—low energy, lack of drive, a general heaviness that creeps into daily life. Doctors look to bloodwork, suspect anemia or thyroid dysfunction, and often come up empty. The problem isn't invisible; it's misdiagnosed. The real cause is not intrinsic energy failure—it's muscular insufficiency. The body isn't tired because it lacks vitality; it's tired because it lacks capacity. What masquerades as fatigue is often weakness in disguise.

The decline in skeletal muscle that begins in midlife doesn't just reduce strength—it increases the cost of movement. Each task becomes metabolically more expensive because the same job is being distributed across fewer, less efficient muscle fibers. Standing from a chair, climbing stairs, carrying groceries— these once-minimal efforts now demand a higher percentage of available strength. The body compensates by reducing output. Not because it's truly out of energy, but because the mechanical cost of basic function has risen above what the muscles can comfortably supply. What used to register as routine now feels exhausting.

This is particularly evident in older adults with no identifiable illness yet persistent complaints of "low energy." Their lab values may be normal, their diets unchanged, and their cardiovascular fitness acceptable. But when examined more closely, their muscle mass has deteriorated, their grip strength is poor, and their lower body force production is well below what's needed for efficient locomotion. This mismatch—between required effort and available strength—is the essence of fatigue that follows no medical diagnosis. It is not systemic failure. It is local underperformance.

The concept of fatigue as a neuromuscular problem is well supported by clinical evidence. A 2016 study in *The Journals of Gerontology* found that self-reported fatigue in older adults strongly correlated with leg strength and power, independent of comorbidities or aerobic capacity. Those in the lowest quintile for strength were significantly more likely to experience day-to-day fatigue, even when adjusting for sleep quality, depression, and cardiovascular status. In other words, the "tired" were not suffering from mystery ailments—they simply lacked force output.

This reframes the typical response to fatigue. Most older adults are told to get more rest, reduce exertion, or pursue stress reduction. Yet these strategies only work if the fatigue is rooted in recovery failure or overstimulation. When the problem is undertraining, more rest only deconditions the system further. The solution isn't less activity—it's more targeted, load-bearing movement. Resistance training restores capacity. It makes daily tasks easier, not by changing the task, but by enlarging the body's reserve to meet it.

This reserve is everything. A strong person climbing stairs uses a fraction of their leg strength. A weak person uses nearly all of it. That difference determines whether the climb feels like exercise or struggle. The stronger individual recovers quickly and maintains stability. The weaker one experiences instability, breathlessness, and lingering fatigue—not because their heart is failing, but because their legs are. This localized deficit reverberates systemically, convincing the brain that the body is exhausted when in fact it is merely insufficient.

The problem compounds over time. As strength drops, the body unconsciously avoids physically demanding tasks. Fewer stairs, shorter walks, more sitting. This conserves energy in the short term but accelerates muscle atrophy. The result is a vicious cycle of weakness begetting fatigue and fatigue justifying further inactivity. What begins as physical underperformance quickly becomes behavioral withdrawal. The brain adapts by recalibrating downward. Tasks that used to be routine become optional. Optional becomes avoided. Avoided becomes impossible.

Breaking this cycle requires direct confrontation with the muscular system. That means resistance training—not cardio, not stretching, not general movement. Cardiovascular exercise does improve endurance, but it does little to rebuild the fast-twitch muscle fibers responsible for power and structural stability. These fibers—Type II—are the ones most lost with age and the ones most essential to reducing perceived effort. A proper strength program targets these fibers through compound lifts and progressive overload, restoring not only physical function but the psychological expectation of effort. Once the body regains the ability to generate force, the experience of fatigue often diminishes without any other intervention.

This is not to say that systemic fatigue doesn't exist. Poor sleep, chronic disease, and medication effects can all sap energy. But these causes are often overstated, while weakness is underestimated. The default assumption in aging should not be that the battery is failing. It should be that the motor has atrophied. And motors can be rebuilt. A 2014 study in *Medicine & Science in Sports & Exercise* showed that adults over sixty who engaged in twelve weeks of strength training reported significant reductions in perceived fatigue, improved mood, and higher physical functioning scores, even though their bodyweight remained unchanged. The intervention worked not by making the body lighter or faster, but by making it stronger.

The body also adapts hormonally to weakness in ways that mimic fatigue. Chronic undertraining reduces anabolic hormone production and increases baseline cortisol. These hormonal shifts promote catabolism, further weakening tissue and impairing recovery. Resistance training reverses this. It upregulates testosterone and growth hormone pathways, lowers resting cortisol, and restores hormonal patterns more closely associated with vigor and vitality. Again, the energy deficit was not primary—it was a reflection of reduced muscular signaling.

Even cognitive fatigue has muscular origins. Executive function is tied to movement capacity. Older adults who lift regularly perform better on memory and problem-solving tasks, likely due to both increased cerebral blood flow and reduced physical stress during activities. If walking through the house or preparing a meal requires conscious effort, mental bandwidth is consumed by physical maintenance. Stronger bodies free the brain to focus on higher-order tasks. In this way, resistance training becomes a cognitive support, not just a physical one.

The broader point is this: most people who feel tired after fifty are not running out of energy—they are operating with insufficient mechanical support. The body is not too old to move. It is too undertrained to do so efficiently. What is experienced as "low energy" is often a muscular deficit disguised as fatigue. It's not the tasks that are harder—it's the engine that has shrunk.

The fix is neither philosophical nor medical. It is physical. Train the legs. Strengthen the back. Load the hips. Improve the capacity to do work, and the perception of effort changes with it. You're not tired. You're weak. And weakness, unlike aging, is optional.

Chapter 11: Why "Toning" Is a Lie

The term "toning" persists in the fitness lexicon like a stubborn myth—vague, unscientific, and deliberately non-threatening. Marketed to aging adults and especially to women, it promises lean, sculpted muscles without the inconvenience of visible effort. No heavy weights, no exertion, no risk of appearing too "bulky." Just light resistance, high reps, and a quietly firm physique. But beneath the surface of this language lies a categorical falsehood: muscles do not tone. They either grow or they atrophy. The illusion of toning is simply the byproduct of two real, measurable processes—hypertrophy and fat loss—both of which require significantly more intensity than the term suggests.

Muscle tone, in clinical terms, refers to the passive tension in a muscle at rest—a neurological property, not a visual one. What most people mean by "toning" is visible muscle definition with minimal size increase. But that look doesn't come from magical shaping or from using pink dumbbells at high repetition. It comes from building enough lean mass to create contour beneath the skin, and reducing fat mass above it. Both processes demand the kind of mechanical tension and metabolic challenge that only proper resistance training can provide. High-rep, low-load routines popularized in group fitness classes or lightweight home circuits are insufficient for either goal. They don't overload the muscle enough to stimulate growth, and they don't elevate energy expenditure enough to drive fat loss meaningfully. The result is wasted time and stagnation disguised as effort.

The appeal of "toning" is that it allows people to train without confronting discomfort. It promises outcomes without visible struggle. But biology does not reward half-measures. Muscle responds to load, not to intention. Without progressive overload—gradually increasing resistance or challenge over time—muscle fibers have no reason to grow or adapt. And without adaptation, nothing changes. The weight becomes a prop, the motion a ritual. That's why so many "toning" routines fail to produce any measurable change in strength, shape, or function.

For aging adults, this matters far more than aesthetic dissatisfaction. After fifty, maintaining or building muscle mass becomes essential for metabolic health, insulin sensitivity, and independence. The strategies required for hypertrophy— challenging weights, full range of motion, controlled eccentrics, and adequate recovery—are not optional for this population. They are foundational. Training with light weights and high repetitions, though occasionally useful for tendon rehabilitation or as an entry point for the severely detrained, is not enough to preserve lean tissue against the tide of age-related sarcopenia. Toning routines that avoid heavy lifting in favor of "lengthening and sculpting" exercises are not benign—they are counterproductive.

The fear that heavier resistance will produce unmanageable muscle bulk is both physiologically unfounded and statistically rare. Hypertrophy requires not just load but adequate volume, high-quality protein intake, recovery, and consistency. Aging bodies, in particular, are less hormonally responsive to training stimuli, a phenomenon known as anabolic resistance. This makes muscle gain slower, not faster. The average adult over fifty, regardless of gender, struggles to build muscle even with well-designed programs. The idea that lifting moderately heavy weights will suddenly create unwanted bulk is not just a misconception—it's a misunderstanding of how difficult hypertrophy actually is, especially post-menopause or in the context of declining testosterone.

This myth is not harmless. It deters people from training in the way their bodies require most. The promise of toning lures them into programs that cannot deliver structural change, metabolic benefit, or lasting improvement. It teaches avoidance of effort. Worse, it reinforces the idea that aging adults—particularly women—should remain physically non-threatening, restrained, and visually modest in their fitness pursuits. It cloaks physical competence in euphemism. The truth is far less marketable: if you want stronger, leaner, more functional muscle after fifty, you have to train hard enough that your muscles are occasionally forced to fail.

There is also the issue of messaging. Toning rhetoric frames fitness as cosmetic maintenance, not as survival. It says, in effect, that your body is a decorative object, not a living machine. For someone trying to regain function, preserve independence, or reverse metabolic decline, this framing is inadequate to the point of negligence. Muscles do not care how you want to look. They respond to demand. If the stimulus is insufficient, the tissue degrades. This is not a philosophical position—it's a biological one.

The reality is that visible muscular definition comes from two intersecting adaptations: muscle hypertrophy and reduction of subcutaneous fat. The first requires progressive resistance training with sufficient load and volume. The second requires either sustained caloric deficit or improved metabolic function—ideally both. Lifting heavier, not lighter, improves insulin sensitivity, increases post-exercise oxygen consumption, and builds the kind of lean tissue that raises basal metabolic rate. In short, the more muscle you have, the more calories you burn doing nothing. This is not a side effect—it is the mechanism. Muscle definition is built under load and revealed through leanness. There is no third path.

Programs that emphasize "long, lean muscle" through stretching or bodyweight movement often misunderstand physiology altogether. Muscle length is determined by the attachment points of tendons and cannot be changed through any amount of light resistance or flexibility work. Muscles can become more flexible and stronger, but they do not elongate like taffy. The appearance of long, lean limbs comes from low body fat and proportional development—not from pulsing with ankle weights in a yoga studio.

Even for those uninterested in aesthetics, the consequences of weak training are functional. The person who trains for tone instead of strength has less muscle, lower bone density, slower reaction time, and poorer balance. They are more likely to fall, less likely to recover, and more vulnerable to joint instability. A leg that cannot press significant weight is not a toned leg—it is a liability in the making. Strength is not just visual; it's structural. And toning, as it is commonly practiced, offers no structure at all.

What's needed instead is a fundamental reframing. Resistance training should not be diluted to accommodate fears of looking too strong. It should be presented as the only effective method for preserving muscle, function, and metabolic health past midlife. That means compound movements, challenging loads, adequate recovery, and progressive demand. If the muscles don't struggle, they won't adapt. And without adaptation, there is no tone—only a slow, quiet descent into fragility disguised as effort.

The truth is simple: toning doesn't exist. It is a marketing term invented to make hard work sound palatable. But palatability does not build muscle. Effort does. And after fifty, effort isn't optional—it's the price of staying upright, independent, and fully capable in a body that no longer maintains itself by default.

Chapter 12: Strength vs. Stamina: What You Really Need

By middle age, most people know they're supposed to "stay active," but few understand what kind of activity their body actually needs to survive the second half of life intact. The default prescription is usually endurance work—walking, cycling, perhaps swimming—because it feels safe, familiar, and virtuous. Stamina becomes the metric: how far can you go, how long can you last, how steady is your heart rate. But what the aging body truly requires is not longer duration—it's greater force. Strength, not stamina, is what preserves autonomy, prevents injury, and extends functional lifespan. And while endurance has its place, it cannot substitute for the biological necessity of muscle.

The difference is more than semantic. Strength is the capacity to generate force against resistance; stamina is the ability to sustain effort over time. The first is what allows you to lift your body off the ground, stabilize yourself during a stumble, or carry weight without compromise. The second allows you to keep moving at submaximal intensity for longer periods. In a younger body, both systems can be built in parallel. But after fifty, recovery slows, anabolic signals weaken, and adaptation becomes a zero-sum game. Time and physiological resources must be spent wisely. Strength pays higher dividends.

Strength declines more rapidly with age than endurance. Studies show that muscle power—how fast you can generate force—diminishes at nearly twice the rate of VO_2 max. This matters because power is what keeps you from falling when you trip, or from collapsing when carrying a heavy object. A 2010 longitudinal study in *The Journal of Gerontology* found that lower body strength predicted mortality, disability, and hospitalization more accurately than any measure of aerobic capacity. You can be able to walk a mile without stopping and still be unable to get off the floor without help. Endurance does not imply resilience.

Endurance training, while beneficial for cardiovascular health, lacks the mechanical loading necessary to stimulate bone remodeling or prevent sarcopenia. Running, unless done at high intensities and with excellent form, often breaks down connective tissue faster than it preserves muscle. Cycling is joint-friendly but almost entirely concentric, offering little eccentric stress to reinforce tendons or improve coordination. Swimming removes gravitational load entirely, making it a poor stimulus for maintaining bone density. In contrast, resistance training loads the skeletal system directly. It provides both axial compression and dynamic tension—the very signals that trigger osteogenesis and maintain muscular integrity.

Moreover, strength training improves cardiovascular health more than commonly acknowledged. Resistance exercise lowers resting blood pressure, improves endothelial function, reduces arterial stiffness, and increases cardiac stroke volume. A 2019 review in *Frontiers in Physiology* found that strength training produced similar, and in some cases superior, improvements in blood pressure and lipid profiles compared to moderate-intensity continuous training. The cardiac adaptations may be different—resistance training builds myocardial strength and ventricular wall thickness, rather than VO_2 max—but they are nonetheless protective. The heart doesn't just need to pump for a long time—it needs to pump forcefully and efficiently under load.

The psychological narrative around stamina reinforces the problem. Phrases like "building endurance" or "pushing through fatigue" frame stamina as noble and strength as optional, even indulgent. But in aging physiology, the opposite is true. Endurance without strength becomes fragility stretched over distance. It allows people to move, but not to lift. It builds motion without resilience. In the absence of muscular power, endurance creates the illusion of competence while leaving the body unprepared for acute stress.

Consider the realities of daily life: carrying groceries, navigating stairs, standing up from a low chair, catching oneself during a slip. None of these demand endurance. All demand strength and coordination. If the legs can't extend with force, or the core can't stabilize under a sudden shift, stamina is irrelevant. In emergency situations, strength is what saves you. No one survives a fall by walking more steps.

Even in clinical populations, the benefits of strength training exceed those of aerobic activity in key outcomes. A 2017 study in *Diabetes Care* found that resistance training was more effective than endurance training at improving insulin sensitivity in older adults with type 2 diabetes. The mechanism is straightforward: muscle is the primary site of glucose disposal. More muscle means more glucose uptake. Strength training also improves posture, mobility, and pain management more effectively than aerobic training, particularly in individuals with arthritis, spinal degeneration, or joint instability—common conditions after fifty.

This does not mean stamina is useless. Aerobic capacity supports mitochondrial health, cognitive function, and cardiovascular endurance. But its return on investment diminishes with age if pursued in isolation. Long bouts of steady-state cardio can also increase cortisol and depress anabolic hormones when not balanced by resistance training. In older adults, this hormonal shift accelerates muscle loss and increases fat storage—precisely what most people are trying to avoid. Without strength, even the benefits of cardio are harder to maintain.

Training for both systems is possible, but the order of operations matters. Strength should come first—both in the weekly schedule and in long-term programming. It sets the foundation for all other forms of movement. Strong muscles make aerobic work more efficient by improving gait mechanics, joint alignment, and overall economy of motion. A body with poor strength will compensate with poor movement patterns during endurance activity, reinforcing dysfunction rather than fitness.

There's also a recovery hierarchy. Strength training, done properly, creates discrete periods of muscular damage and repair. This controlled breakdown prompts growth, adaptation, and increased resilience. Endurance training, especially when overdone, creates systemic fatigue that accumulates without producing new tissue. The older the athlete, the more important it becomes to train in a way that builds rather than just depletes. Strength is additive. Endurance, unmanaged, can be subtractive.

Cultural bias favors stamina because it's easier to measure and romanticize. Running a marathon is a linear achievement. Lifting heavy is nonlinear, unglamorous, and requires technique. It's also slower to build, less intuitive, and more intimidating to those who've spent decades avoiding it. But for the aging body, it is the only path to true physical independence. A 200-pound deadlift does more for long-term survival than an hour on the elliptical ever will.

Ultimately, the question is not how far you can go, but what you can carry, what you can lift, and how well your body resists the gravitational pull of time. Endurance may let you keep moving forward. But strength determines whether you can stand tall, pick yourself up, and keep going after life knocks you down. Aging doesn't reward those who simply last—it rewards those who can still lift.

Chapter 13: The Broken Rehab Model

When older adults get injured—whether from a fall, a joint replacement, or a back strain—the healthcare system funnels them into a rehabilitation process designed more to protect liability than to restore capacity. The protocols emphasize safety, caution, and minimal effective dosing. Physical therapy, as practiced in most clinical settings, becomes a series of isolated movements with resistance bands, balance pads, and three-pound dumbbells. Patients are told to "take it easy," "avoid heavy lifting," and "work within your limits"—phrases that, while well-intentioned, produce the opposite of recovery. They enforce weakness. The modern rehab model, particularly for aging bodies, isn't broken because it fails to heal injuries. It's broken because it refuses to challenge them.

The core failure lies in the refusal to reintroduce progressive overload. Strength does not return through repetition alone—it returns when the tissue is asked to do more than it did yesterday. That principle is foundational in all strength training but conspicuously absent in rehabilitation. After an injury or surgery, therapists will often guide patients through high-rep, low-load movements in the name of "rebuilding function." But function is not reawakened by caution. It's rebuilt by force application that stresses the tissue enough to drive adaptation. Without that load, muscle atrophy accelerates, tendons fail to regain tensile strength, and neuromuscular coordination remains blunted.

Consider the common post-operative knee replacement protocol. Patients are often instructed to perform seated leg extensions with ankle weights, step-ups onto six-inch platforms, and gait training in parallel bars. These movements might restore range of motion or allow for basic walking, but they do not rebuild the quadriceps, glutes, or hamstrings to levels required for stair climbing, fall prevention, or carrying groceries. The leg becomes pain-free but underpowered. Six months later, when the individual trips or attempts to kneel, the strength to stabilize the joint is gone—and so begins the next injury cycle.

This overcautious paradigm stems in part from a legal and insurance-based model of care. Clinicians are disincentivized from pushing patients hard enough to produce adaptation because doing so increases perceived risk, which in turn threatens liability. As a result, they default to conservative movements that are unlikely to injure—but equally unlikely to restore function. Reimbursement is often tied to the number of sessions completed, not the force output regained. So the therapist's goal becomes modest improvement in movement quality, not full restoration of strength or capacity. This creates a system where discharged patients are "recovered" by insurance standards but remain functionally impaired by any meaningful metric.

This conservative approach would make sense if aging tissues were uniquely fragile. But that premise is wrong. While recovery may be slower with age and connective tissue more vulnerable to overload, the adaptive capacity of older adults remains robust when appropriately challenged. Numerous studies have shown that high-load resistance training is not only safe but highly effective in rehabilitating older populations. A 2017 study in *Clinical Rehabilitation* found that older adults recovering from hip fracture who engaged in high-intensity strength training regained walking speed, stair-climbing ability, and lower body strength faster than those in standard physiotherapy. Not only did they avoid re-injury— they became more resilient.

The neuromuscular system in aging adults doesn't stop adapting; it stops receiving adequate stimulus. This matters because muscle loss is not just an inconvenience—it's a risk multiplier. Every week of hospitalization or immobilization can cost an older adult several percent of their lean mass. That loss is not easily regained through light movement. The more time spent in underloaded rehab protocols, the further behind the patient falls. And when they return to real-world conditions—uneven ground, unexpected loads, dynamic balance demands—they are unprepared. Functionally, they've been restored to baseline movement, but not to real-life performance.

The psychological message embedded in rehab is equally damaging. Patients are conditioned to believe that their bodies are fragile, that progress should be slow, and that pain is an enemy to be avoided at all costs. This framing suppresses effort. Instead of building confidence through capability, the rehab model reinforces caution through avoidance. The body adapts not just physically but neurologically to this message. Motor patterns become hesitant. Movement becomes guarded. And effort, the very thing required to rebuild strength, is mentally and emotionally downregulated.

This learned fragility becomes a kind of chronic injury. The original problem heals, but the person moves forward weaker, more cautious, and more dependent on assistive devices or altered mechanics. Even when patients are cleared from therapy, few are transitioned into strength training programs that would reverse the atrophy and rebuild capacity. They're told to "stay active," with no guidance on load progression, intensity, or the difference between movement and training. So they walk, stretch, and do light band work—none of which is sufficient to reverse the strength deficits that caused the injury in the first place.

Contrast this with athletic rehabilitation, where the goal is not just return to play, but return to previous performance. Athletes are not discharged because they can move pain-free; they're discharged when they can produce force, absorb load, and repeat those tasks under fatigue. There is no reason older adults should be held to a lower functional standard—except for the persistent myth that age renders the body non-adaptive. This is not supported by evidence. A 2018 study in *The Journal of Aging and Physical Activity* found that older adults who trained with heavy resistance post-rehabilitation maintained strength gains for months beyond discharge and had lower rates of re-injury than those who followed standard home exercise protocols.

To fix the rehab model, the concept of recovery must be replaced with restoration. Restoration implies a return to prior capacity—or better. That requires lifting real weight, using full ranges of motion, and progressing systematically toward movements that mimic life's demands. Sitting and standing from a chair isn't just a test—it should be a loaded training movement. Walking isn't rehab—it's a baseline expectation. If you can't carry 30 pounds of groceries or climb stairs without bracing yourself, you haven't recovered—you've adapted to limitation.

This shift will not come from insurance companies or regulatory bodies. It must come from patients and practitioners willing to abandon the myth that aging equals fragility. The body doesn't break because it's old—it breaks because it was weak. And weakness isn't repaired by caution. It's reversed by force—applied with intelligence, consistency, and progression.

Rehabilitation that stops at pain-free movement is a failure of both science and imagination. Pain-free is not the goal. Function is. Strength is. Independence is. If the rehab process doesn't rebuild those capacities, then it has not done its job. It has merely postponed the next injury. Aging does not need a gentler approach. It needs a stronger one.

Chapter 14: Mobility Is a Strength Problem

Mobility is often treated as a separate category of fitness—distinct from strength, divorced from load, and addressable through stretching alone. This view is not just incomplete; it is structurally incorrect. For adults over fifty, mobility loss is rarely a flexibility issue. It is a strength deficit. The body does not fail to move because tissues are too tight—it fails to move because it cannot produce or control force through its available range. Mobility, in real terms, is strength expressed at end range. And without load, that expression disappears.

The mistake begins with how mobility is framed. Tight hamstrings, stiff hips, and frozen shoulders are assumed to be limitations of tissue extensibility. The standard prescription is stretching: passive holds, foam rolling, yoga. But these interventions do little to restore movement capacity because they do not address the underlying problem. Muscles don't lengthen usefully unless they are asked to contract through a longer range under tension. Passive range is not the goal. Active, loaded range is. A person who can fold into a hamstring stretch but cannot hinge under load has mobility in theory, but not in practice.

With age, the nervous system becomes increasingly protective. It limits range of motion where strength is insufficient, not to punish, but to preserve. This is a rational adaptation. If the brain doesn't trust the musculature to control a position, it won't allow the body to enter it. That's why so many older adults who stretch religiously still move poorly. They've done nothing to convince the system that those ranges are safe. Mobility, then, is not just a physical state—it's a neurological permission slip. And that permission is earned through strength.

The difference is measurable. A 2017 study in *The Journal of Strength and Conditioning Research* compared traditional stretching protocols with resistance training performed through full range of motion. The latter group showed greater improvements in both flexibility and joint control. This was not because strength training stretched the tissues better—it was because it trained them to produce force at extended lengths. A deep goblet squat, executed with proper form, requires more useful hip and ankle mobility than any static lunge stretch. It builds control where it matters—under load, in motion, through depth.

Older adults often complain of stiffness, but what they are feeling is not always mechanical tension. It is apprehension, neuromuscular hesitation, and poor motor control. Joints that were once fluid now move like rusted hinges not because they've calcified, but because the musculature surrounding them has weakened. Strength training restores this by demanding coordination across multiple joints and ranges. When performed deliberately, it is not just resistance work—it is motor pattern re-education.

The hip is a perfect example. It is a ball-and-socket joint capable of tremendous movement, but in sedentary adults, it becomes locked into a limited range dictated by chair height and walking mechanics. Stretching the hip flexors may provide momentary relief, but it does not restore dynamic function. Loaded lunges, split squats, and kettlebell swings, by contrast, force the hip to move with strength through extension, flexion, and rotation. These movements rebuild capacity—not just the ability to reach the position, but to control and generate force from it.

Shoulders follow a similar pattern. Rounded posture and limited overhead reach are typically blamed on tightness in the pecs or lats, when in reality they stem from weak scapular stabilizers and insufficient thoracic extension strength. Band pull-aparts and passive wall stretches may increase temporary range, but they do not restore the muscular scaffolding needed to sustain movement. Overhead pressing, rows, and loaded carries reintroduce structural integrity to the shoulder girdle. Mobility returns not by pulling on muscles, but by loading them in the positions they were designed to occupy.

The myth of mobility as a passive quality also ignores the role of eccentric strength—the capacity to control the lowering phase of a movement. Aging adults often lose this capacity, leading to jerky transitions, poor braking, and limited positional awareness. Eccentric control is what allows a body to enter a deep squat without collapsing, or to lower from a step without a knee buckle. Resistance training, especially with tempo control, restores this function. It tells the nervous system not only that the range is accessible, but that it's safe.

This redefinition of mobility has implications for fall prevention, injury resilience, and daily performance. An older adult with poor hip mobility will struggle not because their tissues are short, but because their glutes, adductors, and core cannot control the joint under load. A shoulder that won't reach overhead doesn't need to be stretched—it needs to be trained. And a stiff thoracic spine won't respond to foam rolling if the musculature supporting it remains dormant. Motion without strength is ornamental. Strength without motion is incomplete. But strength through motion is functional, durable, and trainable at any age.

Even among experienced exercisers, mobility often gets compartmentalized as something to address before or after "real" training. Warm-ups become a collection of hip openers, ankle drills, and band stretches that bear little resemblance to the movements being trained. But mobility isn't preparatory—it is embedded in the movement itself. A properly executed front squat is a mobility drill. So is a Romanian deadlift, a step-up, or a single-arm overhead press. These movements don't just test mobility—they build it. The tissues adapt to the demands placed on them. If the movement is loaded and controlled, range improves as a byproduct of strength.

The irony is that many of the people most obsessed with mobility are also those who avoid the very loads that would fix it. They fear that tightness means vulnerability, that stiffness is pathological, or that load will aggravate restriction. In reality, well-applied resistance is the antidote to most of these concerns. Muscle fibers realign, joint capsules remodel, and fascial tissues become more responsive when exposed to meaningful tension. Without load, tissues remain passive, disorganized, and neurologically muted.

What emerges from this understanding is a new hierarchy. Stretching is not bad—it's just insufficient. Mobility is not a warm-up goal—it's a strength problem in disguise. And solving it doesn't require more foam rollers, lacrosse balls, or yoga blocks. It requires the willingness to load joints through full, sometimes uncomfortable ranges of motion, repeatedly and with intent. For the aging body, that means not just training harder, but training smarter—understanding that the range you control is the only range that matters.

So the next time you feel "tight," don't just reach for a stretch. Reach for a kettlebell. A barbell. A dumbbell. Train the range you think you've lost. Load it, own it, and repeat it. Because in the end, mobility isn't something you coax out of your body.

It's something you build—under load, over time, and through strength.

Chapter 15: Inflammation and the Anabolic Fix

By the time most people reach their fifties, chronic inflammation has already begun its quiet campaign of biological sabotage. It manifests not through fever or redness, but through slow-burning cellular dysfunction—insulin resistance, joint stiffness, persistent fatigue, and muscle loss that outpaces recovery. This condition, often labeled "inflammaging," is systemic, low-grade, and largely invisible until its downstream consequences—diabetes, heart disease, sarcopenia—start to compound. Conventional medicine responds with anti-inflammatory diets, statins, and nonsteroidal drugs. But these interventions, while symptom-managing, miss the core mechanism of repair. The most powerful anti-inflammatory force available to aging adults isn't pharmacological. It's anabolic. And the primary lever of anabolism after fifty is resistance training.

The idea that lifting weights could suppress inflammation runs counter to popular belief. Many people—especially those managing arthritis or autoimmune conditions—assume that exercise will aggravate symptoms, not alleviate them. But research continues to dismantle this misconception. Strength training, when applied progressively and recovered from appropriately, reduces pro-inflammatory cytokines like IL-6 and TNF-α, increases anti-inflammatory myokines like IL-10 and IL-1ra, and improves immune regulation across multiple systems. In practical terms, this means fewer inflammatory flare-ups, better glucose control, more stable joint function, and enhanced tissue repair. Not through suppression—but through restoration.

The mechanism is elegantly simple. Muscle, when contracted under load, functions as an endocrine organ. It secretes signaling molecules—myokines—that communicate with distant tissues, including the brain, liver, and immune system. Unlike adipokines secreted from fat, which promote inflammation and metabolic dysfunction, myokines like irisin, BDNF, and IL-15 act as anti-inflammatory agents. They inhibit the expression of inflammatory genes, improve insulin sensitivity, and promote mitochondrial biogenesis. In older adults, where both immune function and muscle mass are in decline, this signaling becomes essential. Lifting weights doesn't just build muscle—it signals the body to downregulate its own inflammatory overdrive.

This matters because inflammation and muscle loss are not separate issues. They feed each other. Chronic inflammation accelerates the breakdown of muscle protein by increasing cortisol and suppressing mTOR signaling—the cellular pathway responsible for building new muscle tissue. As lean mass decreases, so does the production of anti-inflammatory myokines, allowing inflammation to escalate further. The result is a catabolic loop: inflammation drives weakness, and weakness removes the very tissue that could suppress inflammation. The only intervention that breaks this loop is anabolic stimulus. And in the context of aging physiology, that stimulus must be mechanical.

A 2019 study in *The Journal of Physiology* demonstrated that older adults who performed resistance training three times per week over twelve weeks saw significant reductions in CRP (C-reactive protein), a key marker of systemic inflammation. These changes occurred even in the absence of weight loss, highlighting that it was the tissue response—anabolism—not caloric deficit, driving the anti-inflammatory effect. This is critical because it reframes inflammation not as something to "cool off" through avoidance or dietary austerity, but something to actively regulate through tissue expansion.

Contrast this with the standard response to inflammation in aging: rest, ice, and avoidance of joint stress. These strategies may reduce acute symptoms, but they reinforce the chronic problem. Inactivity leads to muscle wasting, reduced circulation, joint instability, and increased adiposity—all of which increase systemic inflammation. NSAIDs, meanwhile, blunt pain but also suppress the very cellular pathways involved in muscle repair. Their chronic use, particularly around training, has been shown to impair gains in lean mass and tendon strength. In attempting to mute inflammation pharmacologically, the system becomes less adaptive. What's needed isn't suppression—it's a redirection of the inflammatory signal into tissue repair and growth. Resistance training does exactly that.

This anabolic redirection also improves mitochondrial function, which plays a central role in inflammation. Damaged or senescent mitochondria release reactive oxygen species and activate the NLRP3 inflammasome, a key driver of chronic inflammation. Resistance training, by stimulating mitochondrial turnover and increasing oxidative enzyme activity, improves cellular respiration and reduces mitochondrial-derived inflammatory signaling. In this way, lifting iron repairs not only muscles but the energy systems that sustain them. And as mitochondrial health improves, systemic inflammation recedes—not because the body is avoiding stress, but because it is adapting to it.

Nutrition interacts with this process, but not as the primary driver. High-protein diets rich in leucine support the mTOR pathway, and omega-3 fats modulate inflammatory cascades. Yet without mechanical load, these inputs lack a target. Protein consumed in the absence of training may preserve tissue marginally, but it cannot build new muscle in a system that has lost its sensitivity to growth signals. Anabolic resistance—the blunted muscle-building response to both food and exercise—is a hallmark of aging. Only high-effort strength training has been shown to restore this sensitivity. It doesn't just add muscle—it makes muscle responsive again.

Importantly, this training must be dosed properly. Random motion does not induce the anabolic fix. The anti-inflammatory benefits of resistance training are tightly correlated with intensity and volume. Loads must be sufficient to challenge the muscle, and recovery must be adequate to allow adaptation. Low-resistance, high-rep routines often marketed to aging adults fail to reach the threshold required for meaningful anabolic signaling. They may move blood and lubricate joints, but they do not provoke the hormonal or cellular response necessary to suppress inflammation long-term.

For those dealing with chronic conditions—rheumatoid arthritis, type 2 diabetes, cardiovascular disease—this shift in thinking is urgent. The very pathologies that produce inflammation are the ones most improved by strength training. Resistance work reduces HbA1c levels, lowers blood pressure, improves lipid profiles, and restores vascular function. These are not side effects. They are outcomes. And they result not from pharmacological manipulation but from the restoration of muscle as a regulatory organ.

The broader lesson is this: aging does not inflame the body by default. It inflames the body through disuse, loss of muscle, and lack of mechanical challenge. The immune system, like every other system, becomes dysregulated when the tissue it serves disappears. Strength training restores that tissue. It does not fight inflammation directly—it removes the reasons for its persistence. It tells the body, in a language more powerful than chemistry, that the environment has changed and the system must adapt.

Inflammation is not simply a fire to extinguish. It is a signal to interpret. And the most effective interpretation available after fifty is not rest—it's resistance. The anabolic fix isn't about building mass for its own sake. It's about turning muscle back into a metabolic organ that speaks to the rest of the body in terms it understands. Not through quiet, but through force. Not by avoiding stress, but by applying it wisely, repeatedly, and with purpose.

Chapter 16: Heart Health Doesn't Belong to Runners

For decades, cardiovascular fitness has been synonymous with distance running. The prevailing assumption was simple: to keep the heart healthy, you needed to elevate your heart rate through extended bouts of aerobic activity. Jogging became the prescription. Treadmills and step classes proliferated. Cardiac health, in public imagination and medical advice alike, belonged to the runners. But for adults over fifty, especially those battling declining muscle mass and mounting metabolic dysfunction, this model has aged poorly. The latest evidence doesn't support it. In fact, it undermines it. Heart health, as it turns out, doesn't belong to runners. It belongs to those strong enough to lift.

Cardiovascular disease—the number one cause of death globally—has always been framed as a problem of blood flow, pressure, and plaque. Solutions were drawn accordingly: lower cholesterol, reduce blood pressure, move more. Endurance exercise, because of its clear short-term effects on VO_2 max and resting heart rate, was elevated to near-sacred status. Yet this singular focus ignored the nuanced and cumulative effects of resistance training, which operates through different but equally critical mechanisms. Lifting doesn't just improve the heart's efficiency—it fortifies the body's capacity to manage the stressors that burden the cardiovascular system in the first place.

One of the most misunderstood aspects of cardiac health is the role of skeletal muscle as a mediator of vascular function.

Muscle mass, particularly in the lower body, acts as a vast reservoir for glucose disposal and blood volume regulation. The more muscle an individual has, the more efficiently the body buffers blood sugar, manages lipid profiles, and controls systemic inflammation—all of which are tightly linked to cardiovascular risk. A 2020 meta-analysis in the *British Journal of Sports Medicine* found that individuals who engaged in resistance training two to three times per week had a significantly reduced risk of all-cause and cardiovascular mortality—even when controlling for aerobic activity. In other words, strength alone predicted survival.

This shouldn't be surprising. The heart, after all, is a muscle. It doesn't benefit exclusively from rhythmic endurance—it also responds to pressure. During resistance training, especially with compound lifts, the heart must overcome transient spikes in blood pressure and increased afterload. This stress forces adaptation: improved myocardial contractility, thicker ventricular walls, and greater stroke volume. The heart becomes more powerful, not just more efficient. And unlike endurance training, which largely conditions the cardiovascular system to operate under steady-state demands, resistance training prepares it for variability, sudden spikes, and mechanical tension—the kind of conditions under which most real-world cardiac events occur.

Older adults, in particular, benefit from this hormetic stress. As arteries stiffen with age and baroreceptor sensitivity declines, the ability to tolerate blood pressure fluctuations becomes more important, not less. Strength training increases arterial compliance over time, especially when paired with sufficient recovery and dietary support. A 2018 study in *Hypertension*

Research showed that hypertensive older adults who engaged in a 12-week strength program experienced significant reductions in both systolic and diastolic blood pressure, comparable to the effects seen with first-line antihypertensive medications. These changes were sustained post-intervention, highlighting the remodeling effect of load—not just the temporary dampening of pressure.

There's also the issue of cardiac autonomic balance. As people age, their parasympathetic tone—responsible for rest and recovery—tends to decline, while sympathetic dominance increases. This imbalance contributes to elevated resting heart rate, poor heart rate variability (HRV), and slower recovery from exertion. Resistance training has been shown to improve HRV and reduce resting heart rate, especially when programmed with adequate rest intervals and periodized intensity. The adaptation is not one of mere endurance, but of resilience—better response to stress, faster return to baseline, and more stable cardiac output under variable demands.

In contrast, long-duration aerobic exercise, particularly when performed at moderate intensity without variation, can sometimes induce maladaptive cardiac changes. Endurance athletes with high lifetime mileage show higher rates of atrial fibrillation, left atrial enlargement, and coronary artery calcification. These issues are not universal, but they underscore a simple truth: the cardiovascular system does not benefit from volume alone. It benefits from intelligent stress. And in aging bodies with declining muscle, joint wear, and slower recovery, that stress is more productively applied through lifting than through pounding pavement for miles.

Then there's the metabolic overlay. Most age-related cardiovascular decline is not isolated—it is entangled with insulin resistance, chronic inflammation, and dyslipidemia. Resistance training addresses all three. It improves insulin sensitivity more robustly than cardio alone, particularly in the muscle groups most responsible for glucose clearance: the quads, glutes, and hamstrings. It reduces inflammatory markers not just by decreasing fat mass, but by increasing the production of anti-inflammatory myokines secreted during muscle contraction. And it alters lipid metabolism by shifting the body toward increased fat oxidation and improved triglyceride clearance. None of these benefits require a treadmill. They require progressive overload, sufficient intensity, and recovery.

The cultural elevation of running also ignores its orthopedic cost. Knees, hips, and lower backs that have spent decades under desk-bound compression don't always tolerate the repetitive impact of distance running. Many aging adults, eager to improve cardiovascular health, end up injured, demoralized, or trapped in cycles of pain and recovery. Lifting, when programmed correctly, offers the opposite experience: joints are loaded within controlled ranges, connective tissue is strengthened, and muscle mass protects against instability. The entire system becomes more robust, not more vulnerable. That's not a side benefit. That's the point.

It's also worth noting the psychological impact. Cardiovascular disease isn't just mechanical—it's behavioral. It's tied to mood, stress, adherence, and perceived capability. Resistance training has been shown to improve mental health outcomes, reduce symptoms of depression and anxiety, and improve adherence more than most aerobic interventions. People lift weights and feel stronger. They lift heavier weights and feel more competent. That sense of mastery doesn't just translate to compliance—it becomes a self-reinforcing loop of engagement. Unlike steady-state cardio, which often feels like maintenance, lifting feels like progress.

None of this is to suggest that aerobic activity should be abandoned. A baseline of cardiovascular conditioning supports longevity, endurance, and mitochondrial health. But in aging populations, it must be prioritized beneath strength. A strong person can walk, jog, or cycle if desired. A weak person, no matter how good their aerobic capacity, cannot deadlift, stabilize under load, or recover from a trip. And when the cardiovascular event does come—whether it's climbing stairs, carrying luggage, or surviving a fall—it is strength that predicts outcome, not miles logged.

The heart doesn't care whether you ran a 10K. It cares whether your vascular system can tolerate pressure, whether your muscles can uptake glucose, whether your arteries are supple, and whether your nervous system can recover. These outcomes belong to the lifter. Not because resistance training replaces cardio—but because it addresses the root conditions that make cardiac health possible. In the aging body, where muscle is fading and systems are slowing, the most powerful protection isn't pace—it's power. And the path to power is under the barbell, not on the track.

Chapter 17: The Longevity Muscle: Glutes and Hamstrings

By the time most people enter their fifties, the glutes and hamstrings have become decorative in name only—cosmetically referenced but functionally neglected. These muscles, nestled at the back of the body and chronically undertrained in modern life, are not just support structures. They are the engines of movement, the brakes of balance, and the insurance policy against a devastating fall. They also happen to be among the first to atrophy in sedentary aging, contributing to a cascade of instability, joint degradation, and frailty that no amount of walking or stretching can reverse. If longevity had a muscle group, it would be these: the posterior chain, built to propel and protect. And yet, they're routinely ignored.

The gluteus maximus is the largest muscle in the body, designed to extend the hip with force. It's what allows humans to stand upright, climb, run, rise from a seated position, and maintain balance under shifting loads. The hamstrings, positioned just below, are a triad of long muscles responsible for knee flexion and hip extension. Together, they control the most fundamental movement patterns of daily life: hinging, standing, walking, and stabilizing. In athletic populations, their strength is assumed. In aging populations, their weakness is tolerated. This tolerance is not benign. When the posterior chain fails, the body compensates with dysfunctional patterns—lumbar overextension, anterior pelvic tilt, knee valgus—all of which accelerate joint degeneration and energy inefficiency.

Sarcopenia does not strike all muscles evenly. Type II muscle fibers—the fast-twitch, power-producing units—atrophy first, and these are richly represented in the glutes and hamstrings. That's why one of the earliest signs of aging is not shortness of breath or poor balance, but slowness in rising from a chair. The movement itself is still possible, but the drive—hip extension— has diminished. Instead of pushing with glutes, older adults lean forward, shift weight to the quads, and heave themselves upright using momentum. This compensatory strategy bypasses the very muscles that preserve independence. It also reinforces the decline.

Standard fitness prescriptions for older adults rarely address this. Walking, swimming, and cycling all favor the anterior chain or limit full hip extension. Group classes emphasize knee-dominant patterns or balance drills that float around the problem. Even many weight training programs for seniors focus on machines that isolate muscles without training the integrated function of the posterior chain. The seated leg curl might stimulate the hamstrings in name, but it does nothing to teach them to contract in unison with the glutes during hip extension or to stabilize the pelvis under load. Function is not built in isolation—it is built in patterns.

The consequence of this neglect shows up in every fall-risk profile. Older adults with weak hip extensors are significantly more likely to fall, to fail a sit-to-stand test, or to rely on handrails and momentum for basic transitions. A 2013 study in *The Journals of Gerontology* found that hip extensor strength was one of the strongest predictors of fall risk in adults over sixty-five—more predictive than balance scores or gait speed. The researchers concluded that improving posterior chain strength could be a more effective fall-prevention strategy than traditional balance exercises. In other words, strength—not proprioception—was the missing link.

Moreover, the glutes and hamstrings play a crucial role in spinal health. In the absence of strong hip extensors, the lumbar spine is forced to take on more load than it was designed to handle. Chronic lower back pain, one of the most common complaints in older adults, is often a symptom of this imbalance. The spine is not inherently fragile. It becomes overloaded when primary movers fail to do their job. When the glutes are asleep, the back takes over. When the hamstrings are weak, the pelvis tilts forward, the lumbar curve exaggerates, and disc pressure increases. Rebuilding the posterior chain relieves this burden— not through rest, but through targeted work.

The training solution is not complex, but it is specific. Glute bridges, hip thrusts, Romanian deadlifts, kettlebell swings, and reverse lunges all target the posterior chain with the movement patterns that restore function. These exercises require the hips to extend under load—a pattern missing in most daily life but essential to long-term stability. For older adults, progression must be deliberate. Bodyweight glute bridges may be the starting point, but they cannot be the destination. Load must be added. Range must be controlled. And coordination between glutes and hamstrings must be reinforced through both bilateral and unilateral work.

It's also worth noting that the posterior chain's decline is not simply mechanical—it is behavioral. Sitting, the default posture of modern life, deactivates the glutes and shortens the hip flexors. With each year of sedentarism, the neural pathways to these muscles degrade. They don't just weaken—they forget how to fire. That's why posterior chain training often feels awkward to older lifters. The movement is unfamiliar, the contraction elusive. But this neurological dormancy is reversible. Activation drills, slow eccentrics, and consistent exposure to hip-dominant movement reawaken the signal. Strength follows signal. Function follows strength.

Beyond fall prevention and joint protection, posterior chain training improves gait efficiency and energy conservation. Older adults with stronger hip extensors walk with greater stride length, smoother transitions, and lower metabolic cost. A 2015 study in *Gait & Posture* found that hip extensor strength correlated directly with walking speed and stair-climbing efficiency in adults over sixty. These aren't athletic feats. They're survival tasks. Being able to climb stairs without pain or navigate uneven ground without fear isn't a quality of life enhancement—it's the difference between independence and assisted living.

And yet, this entire muscular system is routinely left out of training programs for older adults. The reasons are cultural as much as technical. The glutes and hamstrings, more than any other muscles, have been sexualized, aestheticized, and trivialized in public discourse. Exercises like the hip thrust are often dismissed as vanity movements, even though their functional benefit far exceeds that of biceps curls or shoulder presses. This bias leads to programs that overtrain the upper body while ignoring the musculature most responsible for upright posture, propulsion, and fall resistance. Aging bodies don't need bigger arms—they need stronger backsides.

The answer is not to abandon cardio, flexibility, or anterior-chain strength. It is to correct the imbalance that modern life and modern training have created. For the aging adult, glute and hamstring work is not a niche concern—it is the center of gravity for physical autonomy. These muscles don't just move you forward. They keep you upright, catch you when you trip, and let you rise after a fall. They are not decorative. They are defensive.

Longevity isn't just about living longer—it's about resisting the forces that try to pull you down before you're ready. Gravity doesn't care about your intentions. Neither does the staircase, the icy sidewalk, or the low chair in the waiting room. The only thing that gets you up, and keeps you up, is strength. And if that strength doesn't come from your posterior chain, then you're relying on borrowed time. The longevity muscle isn't just one muscle. It's a system. And if you want to age on your feet, you'd better start training the back of your body.

Chapter 18: Muscle as an Endocrine Organ

For most of medical history, muscle was regarded as mere machinery—contractile tissue designed to move bones, bear weight, and generate force. It was a mechanical servant of the skeleton, with no inherent regulatory power beyond locomotion. This view persisted even as other organs—like the pancreas, liver, and adipose tissue—were reclassified as endocrine players, communicating across systems through hormones and signaling molecules. Muscle, despite its vast size and metabolic demand, remained silent in that conversation. But the last two decades have rewritten that assumption. Skeletal muscle, especially when contracting under load, is not just reactive—it is communicative. It functions as a powerful endocrine organ, secreting bioactive compounds known as myokines that influence nearly every physiological system. And in aging bodies, this endocrine function becomes the difference between decay and adaptation.

Myokines are cytokines and peptides released by muscle fibers during and after contraction. They enter circulation and interact with distant organs, regulating inflammation, insulin sensitivity, fat metabolism, bone remodeling, and even brain function. The most well-known among them—interleukin-6 (IL-6)—was once dismissed as purely pro-inflammatory, associated with chronic disease. But when secreted by contracting muscle, IL-6 behaves very differently. It initiates anti-inflammatory cascades, stimulates glucose uptake, and activates lipid oxidation. Its context determines its character. From muscle, it signals adaptation. From adipose tissue, it signals dysfunction.

This distinction is crucial because muscle-derived IL-6 and similar myokines do not operate in isolation. They modulate entire networks of hormonal and immune activity. For aging adults, whose hormonal profiles and immune responses are already in decline, the endocrine function of muscle becomes essential. Resistance training, by triggering the release of these signaling molecules, doesn't just build tissue—it restores systemic communication. It tells the immune system to recalibrate, the brain to engage in neuroplasticity, and the pancreas to become more insulin-sensitive. It transforms skeletal muscle into a metabolic control center.

Consider irisin, another myokine secreted during exercise. It's been shown to promote browning of white adipose tissue—

converting it from an inert fat store to a metabolically active tissue that burns energy. This shift improves energy expenditure and supports weight regulation, particularly in individuals with reduced resting metabolic rates due to aging or sarcopenia. Resistance training, especially at moderate to high intensity, enhances irisin secretion more than aerobic exercise. The implication is that muscle contraction doesn't just burn calories—it alters the metabolic character of other tissues in ways that make long-term fat regulation more sustainable.

Then there's brain-derived neurotrophic factor (BDNF), another molecule released during muscular work. BDNF supports synaptic plasticity, learning, and memory—functions that decline with age and are increasingly linked to neurodegenerative disease. While traditionally associated with aerobic activity, recent studies show that resistance training, particularly when performed with compound movements and coordination demands, also stimulates BDNF production. The mechanism is partly indirect: myokines like cathepsin B and irisin cross the blood–brain barrier and trigger BDNF expression within the brain. The practical result is cognitive preservation through muscular activation—not just through blood flow, but through biochemical signaling.

This muscle–brain axis helps explain why strength correlates so strongly with cognitive outcomes. Multiple longitudinal studies have found that grip strength, leg press strength, and total lean mass are predictive of executive function, memory, and dementia risk. These aren't just correlative markers—they reflect an active dialogue between muscle and the central nervous system, maintained by movement and load. When muscle atrophies, that conversation falls silent. What follows isn't just physical decline—it's neural impoverishment. Training reinitiates the exchange.

Even the skeletal system responds to myokine signals. Muscle and bone are not just mechanically linked—they're hormonally co-regulated. Myokines like IGF-1 (insulin-like growth factor) and MGF (mechano growth factor) stimulate osteoblast activity, increasing bone formation in response to mechanical load. This endocrine communication complements the mechanical stress applied through resistance training, amplifying bone density gains and reducing osteoporosis risk. It also explains why strength training is more effective for bone health than passive calcium supplementation or bisphosphonates. It activates the tissue, both physically and chemically.

The immune system, too, is recalibrated by myokines. Contracting muscles reduce levels of TNF-α and IL-1β—key pro-inflammatory cytokines implicated in chronic disease— and increase levels of IL-10 and IL-1ra, which suppress inflammatory responses. This anti-inflammatory effect is not just local. It circulates systemically, reducing the burden of low-grade chronic inflammation that underlies metabolic syndrome, cardiovascular disease, and even cancer progression. In older adults, where immunosenescence weakens response and increases baseline inflammation, the myokine cascade becomes essential. It doesn't require medication. It requires mechanical tension, applied consistently, across full ranges of motion.

This reframing of muscle as an endocrine organ also repositions the conversation around exercise. The benefits of resistance training are not confined to strength or hypertrophy. They ripple outward, improving hormonal profiles, immune regulation, organ function, and neural integrity. Muscle is not passive—it is proactive. And unlike pharmacological interventions, which often target single pathways, strength training engages multiple systems simultaneously. It doesn't manage disease—it restores function.

For aging adults, this matters more than ever. Hormonal decline, reduced mitochondrial efficiency, and inflammatory drift aren't inevitable consequences of time. They are signals of disuse. A sedentary body stops speaking to itself in the language of adaptation. Myokine production diminishes. Insulin sensitivity drops. Fat accumulates. Neurons retract. Bones weaken. The fix is not a pill—it is permission for the body to challenge itself. Every loaded rep is a hormonal broadcast, telling the entire system that the environment still demands effort. And where there is demand, there is repair.

None of this happens through casual movement. Walking, while valuable for cardiovascular maintenance and mood, does not produce the intensity required to activate the full myokine cascade. Nor does passive stretching, or light band work, or chair-based exercise routines marketed to seniors. What's needed is muscular contraction against real resistance—load that forces recruitment, tension, and fatigue. It doesn't require maximal effort, but it does require intention. The body knows when it's working. And only when it works hard enough does it begin to speak biochemically.

Understanding muscle as an endocrine organ shifts the goalposts. Strength is no longer just about load capacity. It's about biochemical influence. It's about maintaining communication between systems that, in the absence of muscle, fall into entropy. The loss of muscle is not just a loss of tissue—it's a silencing of regulatory feedback that keeps the body coherent.

So, yes, muscle lifts weight. But it also lifts mood, regulates inflammation, processes glucose, defends bone, and preserves cognition. It secretes, signals, and sustains. It is, in every sense, an organ. And in a body over fifty, where systemic resilience starts to erode, the only way to keep the lines of communication open is through contraction under load. Muscle must speak—and lifting is its voice.

Chapter 19: Why Your Doctor Doesn't Tell You This

When a fifty-five-year-old walks into a physician's office complaining of fatigue, joint pain, creeping weight gain, or blood sugar dysregulation, the response typically follows a predictable script: bloodwork, a statin or metformin, maybe a referral to a dietitian, and vague encouragement to "get more exercise." But almost never will the doctor say: start strength training, load your posterior chain, reverse-engineer sarcopenia through progressive resistance. This omission isn't born of negligence or malice. It's structural. Your doctor doesn't tell you this because, in most cases, they were never taught. Exercise prescription, particularly resistance training, remains a blind spot in medical education—an evidence-rich but curriculum-poor frontier that medicine still treats as peripheral.

Medical school, by design, is a triage education. It is built to diagnose, categorize, and manage pathology through pharmacological and procedural means. In that context, prevention often plays second fiddle to treatment. Of the roughly 20,000 hours that comprise medical training, fewer than 1% are devoted to physical activity, and even less to strength-specific modalities. When movement is discussed, it's usually under the umbrella of cardiovascular health, with a brief nod to aerobic conditioning and BMI reduction. Lifting weights—especially as a first-line intervention for insulin resistance, bone loss, mood disorders, or age-related decline—is almost never framed as medicine.

The result is a profession that excels at identifying disease but struggles to prescribe function. Physicians are trained to monitor blood pressure but not to interpret a squat. They can diagnose osteopenia but rarely understand how deadlifts rebuild bone. They can chart sarcopenia on a DEXA scan but are rarely trained in the loading protocols that reverse it. And so, even when strength loss is identified as a clinical issue, the solution defaults to lifestyle platitudes: eat better, move more, take your meds. This is not guidance. It's abdication, dressed in good intentions.

Ironically, the data supporting resistance training as medical intervention is not fringe—it's voluminous. A 2014 review in *Diabetes Care* showed that progressive strength training significantly improves HbA1c and insulin sensitivity in older adults, often more effectively than aerobic exercise. A 2017 meta-analysis in *Osteoporosis International* concluded that high-intensity resistance training was more effective than pharmacological treatments at improving bone mineral density in postmenopausal women. And studies in *The Journal of the American Geriatrics Society* have repeatedly shown that muscle strength, particularly in the legs, predicts mortality, fall risk, and hospitalization rates more accurately than traditional cardiovascular markers. This isn't speculation—it's a blind spot that has become indefensible.

Part of the problem is that medicine treats strength training as a lifestyle choice, not a clinical tool. Doctors do not hesitate to prescribe exercise for cardiac rehab, yet rarely prescribe it to prevent the very events that require that rehab. The threshold for intervention is too high—patients must fail before training is prescribed. And when it is, the referral is often to physical therapy or general fitness programs that avoid the very thing that produces adaptation: load. The patient ends up stretching bands in a clinical office, not squatting under weight. The result is motion without resistance, and resistance without progression—an elegant way to waste time.

Cultural bias also plays a role. Strength training is still culturally coded as athletic, aggressive, or male-dominated. It's associated with performance, not preservation. Many older patients—and their doctors—view lifting as something best left to bodybuilders, not a clinical modality suitable for a seventy-year-old with osteopenia and borderline glucose control. This misunderstanding creates a feedback loop of avoidance: patients don't ask, doctors don't prescribe, and the decline accelerates.

Even when physicians are personally aware of the benefits of strength training, the system does little to support their implementation. Clinic schedules are compressed. Reimbursement models favor procedures and pharmacology over patient education. Few doctors have access to allied professionals trained to deliver resistance-based interventions.

And so even those inclined to recommend lifting often default to generalities—"do some resistance work"—leaving patients to navigate the vast, confusing world of gyms, trainers, and Instagram pseudo-experts on their own.

The consequences of this gap are not abstract. Millions of aging adults are being managed for preventable conditions with chronic medication regimens instead of muscle. Sarcopenia is treated as inevitable rather than modifiable. Fractures from falls are addressed with surgery rather than strength. Cognitive decline is mourned rather than mitigated. In many cases, the correct first intervention isn't a pill. It's a barbell.

Contrast this with how strength is viewed in sports medicine or elite performance. In those settings, resistance training is foundational, not optional. It's programmed with precision, tracked like a biomarker, and adjusted based on performance metrics. The question isn't whether to train—it's how to optimize. There is no confusion over its value. The only mystery is why that clarity vanishes the moment the client is over fifty and has a Medicare card.

The irony is that older adults often respond better to strength training than younger populations—because the gap between baseline and potential is wider. Improvements in strength, coordination, mood, metabolic function, and bone density can be dramatic even with modest loading. These gains are not just measurable—they're transformative. They reduce polypharmacy, improve independence, and extend functional lifespan. No drug on earth does all that with fewer side effects. Yet resistance training remains under-prescribed, under-respected, and underfunded in primary care.

This is not an indictment of individual physicians. It is an indictment of a system that separates physiology from movement, adaptation from medicine, and prevention from practice. Doctors are not at fault for what they were never taught. But the gap must be closed. Muscle is not a luxury—it is an organ of survival. And every year of unchallenged muscle loss is a year closer to decline, dependency, and death. The tools to reverse this are simple: load, progression, recovery, consistency. But they must be initiated, not just tolerated.

Until resistance training becomes as routine in medical prescriptions as blood pressure checks or lipid panels, the problem will persist. Not because we lack knowledge, but because we've failed to translate it into action. Your doctor doesn't tell you this not because it's wrong—but because, in many ways, they still think like a pharmacologist, not a physiologist. It's time they caught up. Aging isn't a disease. But muscle loss is a treatable condition. And the medicine is already in your hands. Or more accurately, in your legs, your hips, and your back. You just have to lift it.

Chapter 20: The Sarcopenia-Obesity Loop

Sarcopenia and obesity are often treated as separate conditions—one the slow wasting of muscle with age, the other the accumulation of excess fat. But in adults over fifty, these are not parallel issues; they are synergistic pathologies locked in a feedback loop. Muscle loss accelerates fat gain, and fat gain exacerbates muscle loss. This vicious cycle, known as sarcopenic obesity, is far more destructive than either condition alone. It doesn't just compromise aesthetics or strength—it reshapes metabolism, degrades insulin sensitivity, and increases mortality risk with a stealth few clinicians are trained to catch. And once the loop takes hold, it cannot be broken with calorie restriction or cardio alone. Resistance training is the only intervention that addresses both ends of the problem.

Muscle is metabolically expensive. It consumes energy even at rest, contributes to glucose uptake, and secretes anti-inflammatory myokines that support hormonal balance and fat oxidation. As muscle declines, the body's ability to manage blood sugar, burn calories, and regulate inflammation collapses in parallel. This creates a metabolic vacuum—energy that was once partitioned toward active tissue is now stored in adipose depots, especially visceral fat, the kind that wraps around internal organs and drives systemic disease. Meanwhile, fat tissue, particularly in excess, secretes pro-inflammatory cytokines like TNF-α and IL-6 in their damaging form, creating a chronic inflammatory environment that further inhibits muscle protein synthesis.

This is not just a matter of poor diet or low activity. It is a biological drift that begins subtly, often before it's noticed. In the fifth and sixth decades, people frequently report weight gain without eating more. Clothes tighten, energy dips, waistlines expand—but the scale may not shift dramatically. That's because fat is replacing muscle gram for gram. Total weight remains stable, masking the underlying body composition change. This recomposition erodes strength, stability, and metabolic function even before BMI thresholds flag concern. By the time it's diagnosed, sarcopenic obesity has already diminished resilience across every system.

The hormonal environment accelerates this process. Declining testosterone and estrogen levels reduce the body's natural anabolic drive. Insulin resistance, fueled by fat accumulation, blunts nutrient partitioning into muscle. Cortisol, often elevated in chronic stress or poor sleep, further encourages catabolism. The older body becomes primed to store and disinclined to build. Under these conditions, the typical prescription—cut calories and walk more—is not just ineffective; it is counterproductive. Calorie restriction without resistance training reduces weight, but the weight lost is disproportionately lean mass. The less muscle there is, the harder fat becomes to lose. The loop tightens.

A 2010 study in *The American Journal of Clinical Nutrition* demonstrated that older adults who lost weight through diet alone saw significant reductions in lean mass, bone density, and resting metabolic rate. When the same intervention was paired with strength training, not only was muscle preserved—it was gained in some cases, and fat loss was more pronounced. The message is clear: weight loss in aging adults must be resistance-guided, not just scale-focused. Without a muscle-preserving stimulus, the body cannibalizes itself, shrinking the very tissue that keeps metabolism healthy.

This is where resistance training breaks the loop. It stimulates muscle protein synthesis, even in anabolic-resistant older adults, when performed with sufficient load and frequency. It improves insulin sensitivity by increasing GLUT-4 transporter activity in muscle cells. It reduces inflammatory markers through myokine release. It elevates resting metabolic rate by expanding metabolically active tissue. And perhaps most critically, it reinforces the neurological patterns that prevent mobility loss and the sedentary spiral that drives fat accumulation. Lifting doesn't just build muscle—it restores the body's capacity to partition energy properly, fight inflammation, and stay active without effort becoming punitive.

Importantly, the effects of strength training on fat loss are not always captured by the scale. A person may maintain or even gain weight while radically improving their body composition. Waist circumference shrinks. Blood markers normalize. Glucose becomes easier to manage. But because many adults remain fixated on total body weight, they miss the deeper transformation. This is especially dangerous when the goal is to "lose weight" after middle age. Without reframing the objective as fat loss with muscle retention or gain, the typical approach— eat less, move more—results in a weaker, slower, and more metabolically compromised version of the same person.

Visceral fat also has a unique relationship with muscle loss. Unlike subcutaneous fat, which is largely inert, visceral adiposity directly impairs muscle function. It increases oxidative stress, floods the system with inflammatory signals, and contributes to mitochondrial dysfunction in muscle cells. The presence of this fat accelerates sarcopenia, which then reduces the capacity to burn it off. It becomes a biochemical tug-of-war that no amount of walking or dietary fiber can resolve. Only by rebuilding the muscle machinery responsible for oxidizing fat and regulating hormones can the loop be disrupted.

Behavioral inertia compounds the physiological trap. As people gain fat and lose muscle, movement becomes harder. Joints ache. Stamina drops. Exercise feels punishing instead of invigorating. The activities that once kept weight stable—recreational sports, spontaneous movement, even long walks—become less accessible. Sedentarism sets in, not as a choice but as a biomechanical inevitability. Resistance training changes this not just by increasing strength, but by making movement feel easier. The stronger the musculature, the less taxing daily life becomes. This lowers the barrier to non-exercise activity, which in turn supports healthier energy balance.

The loop is further reinforced by social and medical messaging. Fat is visible and therefore targeted. Muscle is invisible until it's gone. Patients are told to lose weight, but rarely told to build strength. Doctors monitor cholesterol and blood pressure, but not grip strength or gait speed. Fitness programs for aging adults emphasize movement quality and flexibility while neglecting hypertrophy. The result is a focus on symptoms rather than cause. We treat fat like the disease and ignore the erosion of the one tissue that makes fat manageable: muscle.

Breaking the sarcopenia-obesity loop is not a matter of intention. It is a matter of stimulus. The body will not hold onto muscle without reason. Protein intake alone won't build it. Cardio alone won't preserve it. Only mechanical tension against progressive load sends the signal that muscle matters. And once that signal is sent consistently, the entire system starts to recalibrate. Glucose clearance improves. Inflammation subsides. Energy returns. Fat becomes easier to lose—not because of deprivation, but because the machinery to burn it is back online.

Sarcopenic obesity is not a niche condition. It is the unspoken norm in aging populations. But it is not inevitable. The loop can be broken—not by targeting fat, but by rebuilding muscle. Not by eating less, but by training more intelligently. Strength is not the opposite of obesity. It is the antidote to the conditions that make obesity inevitable. And in bodies over fifty, where every year without muscle is a year of diminished return, lifting is not a fitness strategy. It is metabolic triage.

Chapter 21: You Can't Diet Your Way to Strength

The belief that fat loss equates to health gain has been deeply ingrained in public consciousness. Caloric restriction is held up as the universal solution to middle-age spread, while strength is treated as an optional add-on—something to be pursued once the "real" work of dieting is done. But this order of operations is not just misguided. It's metabolically backwards. After fifty, the margin for error narrows. The body becomes less forgiving, more prone to catabolism, and increasingly resistant to rebuilding. In this context, dieting without resistance training is not just ineffective—it's destructive. You cannot diet your way to strength, because the loss of muscle, once accelerated, is rarely reclaimed without deliberate mechanical stimulus.

Calorie restriction, by design, initiates tissue loss. The body cannot differentiate between expendable fat and essential lean mass without a signal. In younger individuals, the hormonal environment is favorable enough to preserve muscle even in deficits. Testosterone, growth hormone, and protein turnover remain elevated. But after fifty, these systems begin to downshift. Without an anabolic counterbalance, the body readily consumes its own muscle to meet caloric shortfall. This erosion isn't theoretical—it's quantifiable. Studies repeatedly show that weight lost through diet alone consists of up to 30% lean mass, particularly in older adults whose musculature is already diminished.

The result is a leaner but weaker individual, metabolically disadvantaged and more prone to regain fat once the diet ends. This phenomenon, often mislabeled as "yo-yo dieting," is less about psychological lapses and more about biological sabotage. Muscle drives resting metabolic rate, supports insulin sensitivity, and mediates hormonal balance. Strip it away, and the body burns fewer calories, stores more fat, and becomes less responsive to satiety cues. Each subsequent attempt at dieting becomes harder, and the body less cooperative. The scale may fluctuate, but the net effect is regression, not progress.

Protein intake, while important, cannot solve this problem in isolation. Dietary protein provides the raw material for repair, but not the signal to build. That signal comes from load—progressive, mechanical tension placed across muscle fibers. Without that stimulus, even high-protein diets result in nitrogen excretion, not lean mass accretion. Resistance training activates mTOR signaling, recruits satellite cells, and initiates the microdamage necessary to provoke adaptation. It tells the body that muscle is still needed, that it cannot be sacrificed to caloric efficiency. This signal is non-negotiable. It must be present, especially in calorie deficits.

This is why any weight-loss strategy over fifty must prioritize strength training as its foundation—not an accessory to be added after fat is lost, but the central behavior around which diet is built. The goal is not to lose weight quickly but to lose fat selectively while preserving or increasing lean mass. This approach, often called body recomposition, is slower but far more sustainable. It avoids the metabolic downregulation that haunts crash diets and ensures that fat loss does not come at the cost of function.

Moreover, lifting while dieting offers psychological leverage. Traditional dieting often feels like deprivation: fewer meals, smaller portions, social friction. Strength training introduces a counter-narrative of capability. Instead of shrinking the body passively, the lifter builds something actively. This changes the emotional tone of the entire process. Muscle becomes not a side effect to be minimized but the target. Performance improves even as the scale moves slowly, anchoring progress to strength, not aesthetics. For aging adults, who often feel trapped between decline and cosmetic pressure, this reframing is essential.

The cultural obsession with thinness also obscures the importance of load-bearing capacity. A 130-pound woman who cannot squat her own bodyweight is not healthier than a 150-pound woman who can. The former is light but fragile. The latter is heavier but resilient. When the inevitable challenges of aging arrive—falls, illness, hospitalizations—it is the stronger body that recovers faster, resists atrophy, and returns to baseline. Strength is not decorative. It is biological infrastructure. And that infrastructure cannot be built through diet.

This becomes even more urgent in the context of sarcopenia. Muscle loss after fifty occurs at an average rate of 1–2% per year, with strength declining up to 3% annually. Calorie restriction accelerates both trajectories. Once critical thresholds are crossed—such as difficulty rising from a chair or walking up stairs—the decline often becomes exponential. No amount of weight loss offsets the functional losses that result. In this light, dieting without lifting is not neutral—it's degenerative.

A 2016 study in *Obesity Reviews* compared older adults undergoing calorie restriction alone versus those combining it with resistance training. The exercise group preserved significantly more lean mass, had better insulin sensitivity, and retained more functional independence. Their metabolic rate remained higher, and fat regain post-intervention was lower. These are not marginal gains—they are the difference between surviving aging and being crushed by it.

It's also worth dismantling the idea that one must "earn the right" to lift by first losing weight. This sequence, commonly pushed in weight-loss clinics and fitness marketing, reflects a misunderstanding of both physiology and psychology. Heavy individuals often gain strength quickly when they begin lifting, thanks to pre-existing mass and leverage advantages. These early neurological and muscular adaptations build confidence, competence, and adherence—all essential for sustained change. Delaying this engagement in favor of prolonged dieting deprives them of these wins and increases dropout rates. The iron should be introduced early—not as a reward, but as a requirement.

The argument that lifting is dangerous for heavier or older individuals also fails under scrutiny. When scaled appropriately and supervised, resistance training is safer than most aerobic activity. It can be performed without impact, tailored to joint limitations, and progressed at a pace that matches recovery. It reinforces connective tissue, improves balance, and builds proprioception—all of which reduce injury risk in everyday life. Compared to chronic dieting, which often leads to fatigue, nutrient deficiencies, and disordered eating patterns, lifting is not risky. It is restorative.

The fixation on dietary purity—low-carb, low-fat, intermittent fasting—also obscures the essential variable: muscle preservation. No nutritional protocol can compensate for the absence of mechanical tension. Keto without training leads to lean mass loss. Fasting without resistance results in strength loss. These dietary tools, when used, must be structured around the primary goal: maintaining or increasing the muscle that anchors metabolic health. Otherwise, they are just different roads to the same dead end.

The takeaway is clear: if you are over fifty, your primary concern is not how little you can eat—it's how much strength you can retain. Weight loss, if it happens, should be incidental to that process. The body does not care how lean you are if you are too weak to stand up from the floor or carry groceries up stairs. Strength is what defends against disease, maintains independence, and improves quality of life. And no deficit, however meticulously calculated, can build it in your absence from the weight room.

Dieting may make you smaller. Only training makes you stronger. And past a certain age, smaller is not better if it means slower, softer, and less resilient. In the war against aging, calories are currency—but strength is survival.

Chapter 22: The Wrong Way to Lose Weight Over 50

The prevailing approach to weight loss in people over fifty is still stuck in a paradigm built for youth and vanity. Cut calories, do more cardio, watch the scale. The strategy, while superficially effective, is metabolically reckless. It treats body fat as the sole enemy and ignores the critical role of muscle in regulating weight, preserving function, and sustaining health. For aging adults, losing weight the wrong way doesn't just fail—it accelerates decline. The damage is not always visible on the surface, but under the skin, in bone, muscle, and hormone levels, the cost is devastating. And the worst part? Most people think they're doing everything right.

After fifty, the body undergoes a subtle but accelerating shift toward catabolism. Hormones that once promoted muscle retention—testosterone, estrogen, growth hormone—begin to taper. Protein synthesis slows. Mitochondria falter. In this environment, muscle becomes expensive to maintain and easy to lose. The typical diet-first approach to weight loss—cutting calories without concurrent strength training—doesn't account for this. It assumes the body will shed fat preferentially. But biology doesn't work that way. The body sheds what it no longer perceives as essential. Without resistance, that means muscle goes first.

This is where the common mistake begins: assuming the number on the scale reflects progress. In middle age and beyond, scale weight becomes a deeply misleading metric. You can lose ten pounds and become less metabolically healthy. You can reduce your BMI and increase your risk of fracture. You can slim your waistline and simultaneously cripple your ability to rise from a chair. None of this appears in the mirror, but it will show up in your labs, in your blood sugar, in your balance, in your stamina. The pounds come off, but so does your capacity to live without dependence.

A 2008 study in *The American Journal of Clinical Nutrition* examined the effects of caloric restriction in older adults and found that while participants lost weight, up to 35% of that loss came from lean mass. Worse, much of that lean mass was not regained even after returning to normal calorie intake. Instead, fat mass crept back in. This created a condition researchers dubbed "weight cycling-induced sarcopenia"—a slower, softer, metabolically compromised version of the person who had initially dieted. The short-term weight loss goal had been achieved, but at the cost of long-term resilience.

The obsession with low numbers and smaller bodies is a cultural artifact, not a medical directive. Medical providers, too often governed by BMI charts and insurance targets, reinforce this bias by praising weight loss without asking how it was achieved. But the method matters. A body that is weak, brittle, and energy-starved is not a healthier body, even if it fits into smaller clothes. Muscle is not vanity tissue. It is the largest site of glucose disposal, the most modifiable element of resting metabolic rate, and the primary protector against frailty. Losing it for the sake of a smaller scale reading is not sacrifice— it's sabotage.

The wrong way to lose weight also includes the overuse of steady-state cardio. Hours on the treadmill or elliptical, often combined with low-calorie diets, are a recipe for muscle degradation. Cardio burns calories, yes, but in a low-hormonal environment and a caloric deficit, the body breaks down muscle to keep the engine running. The endurance adaptations gained are limited in older adults compared to younger individuals, and the orthopedic toll—on joints, tendons, and connective tissue—is greater. This creates a paradox: the very method used to "get healthy" may be worsening the structural integrity needed for longevity.

Resistance training, in contrast, sends the opposite message. It tells the body that muscle is necessary. When performed with appropriate intensity, it upregulates anabolic signaling, increases protein turnover, and improves the hormonal environment, even in calorie deficits. Muscle isn't spared passively—it's defended actively. Weight loss still occurs, but it happens more slowly, more selectively, and more meaningfully. Fat decreases. Muscle remains—or, with careful programming, even increases. The scale moves less dramatically, but the mirror and the labwork tell a different story.

There is also the issue of dietary composition. Many popular weight-loss strategies—low-fat, low-carb, intermittent fasting—place more emphasis on restriction than on muscle preservation. Protein intake in aging adults is often insufficient, both in quantity and distribution. The recommended dietary allowance of 0.8 grams per kilogram of body weight is a minimum, not a target—and wholly inadequate for someone trying to lose fat while maintaining lean mass. Most older adults need closer to 1.2 to 1.6 grams per kilogram, spread evenly across meals, to support muscle protein synthesis in the context of aging and training. Anything less, and the body defaults to cannibalizing muscle.

The wrong way to lose weight over fifty also includes a psychological trap: chasing quick results. Middle age comes with urgency—people feel the clock ticking, the joints aching, the clothes tightening. This urgency often pushes people into unsustainable, high-restriction programs that yield short-term drops and long-term rebounds. The problem isn't willpower—it's physiology. The body defends against perceived starvation by downregulating energy expenditure, increasing hunger hormones, and becoming more efficient at storing fat. Without concurrent strength training to maintain muscle and elevate metabolic demand, the rebound is almost guaranteed.

Even successful weight loss, when done without muscle focus, can have unintended consequences. Bone density often drops alongside lean mass in caloric deficits, especially in postmenopausal women. This increases fracture risk at precisely the stage of life when recovery is slowest. Sarcopenic individuals are also more vulnerable to falls, infections, and hospitalizations. What appears as a smaller, "healthier" body can, in fact, be a frailer one—thinner, yes, but more breakable, more glucose-intolerant, and less resilient to physiological stress.

So what does the right approach look like? It doesn't begin with calorie cuts. It begins with load—resistance training that stimulates the muscle to stay. Diet follows, and it does so in service to strength. Protein is prioritized. Deficits are moderate. Progress is measured in waistlines and lifts, not just pounds. And the timeline is longer—not six weeks, but six months or more. This process is slower, but it is corrective. It doesn't just reduce weight—it improves tissue quality, metabolic health, and physical capacity.

The wrong way to lose weight over fifty is to treat fat as the only problem. The right way is to recognize that strength is the foundation of sustainable change. Without muscle, every pound lost is a liability. With muscle, every pound lost becomes an asset. The scale can no longer be trusted as a compass. The body must be measured by what it can do, not just how much it weighs.

After fifty, you're not just managing calories. You're managing tissue integrity, hormonal stability, and long-term independence. That demands a better metric, a better process, and above all, a better priority. The number one goal isn't weight loss. It's muscle retention. Get that right, and the rest will follow. Lose the wrong weight, and you're only setting yourself up for a harder, heavier rebound—one the body may not be strong enough to fight next time.

Chapter 23: Stress, Cortisol, and Lifting as Therapy

By the time most adults reach their fifties, stress is no longer an occasional surge—it's a chronic undercurrent. Financial pressures, aging parents, children leaving or returning home, declining health, unstable sleep, and an increasing awareness of mortality all converge into a hormonal landscape dominated by cortisol. The body, finely tuned over millennia to handle short bursts of stress through fight-or-flight responses, now spends most of its time in a low-grade simmer of tension. Cortisol, once adaptive, becomes corrosive. It shrinks muscle, stores fat, disrupts sleep, impairs cognition, and raises blood pressure. And yet, most advice about stress management remains anchored in breathwork and vague appeals to "mindfulness." What gets overlooked is that muscle—specifically, lifting heavy things—might be the most effective tool for regulating cortisol and restoring hormonal equilibrium in the aging body.

Cortisol is not inherently bad. In acute doses, it mobilizes energy, enhances alertness, and facilitates survival. It rises in the morning to wake the brain, peaks during exertion, and drops when the stressor ends. The problem begins when the stressor never ends. Chronic elevation of cortisol flattens its natural rhythm, leading to persistent catabolism, impaired glucose metabolism, and immune suppression. In older adults, the consequences are exaggerated. Lean mass evaporates faster. Visceral fat accumulates. Recovery slows. Sleep becomes fragmented. Cognitive sharpness dulls. It's not burnout in the metaphorical sense—it's burnout in the literal endocrine sense.

This is where resistance training flips the script. While a single bout of intense lifting can transiently elevate cortisol—as any stressor would—it simultaneously trains the body to recover faster, reset more efficiently, and restore a healthier hormonal rhythm. Regular resistance training improves the body's resilience to stressors, both physical and psychological. It enhances parasympathetic tone, reduces baseline cortisol levels, and increases the capacity of the hypothalamic-pituitary-adrenal (HPA) axis to respond appropriately. In simpler terms: the system becomes better at handling stress, rather than drowning in it.

A 2010 study in *Psychoneuroendocrinology* found that participants engaged in regular resistance training exhibited significantly lower resting cortisol levels than sedentary controls. Not only that, but their post-stress recovery—

measured by heart rate variability and cortisol clearance—was markedly faster. This is not a fluke. It's part of a pattern repeatedly observed in clinical trials: the trained body doesn't just handle physical demands better; it handles emotional volatility better, too.

It's important to distinguish the kind of training that produces this effect. Low-effort, low-intensity movement lacks the physiological gravity to rewire hormonal responses. The training must be progressive. It must include compound lifts. It must require effort, focus, and adaptation. What distinguishes lifting from other forms of exercise is its demand on the entire neuromuscular system. That demand provokes not just muscular change, but systemic recalibration—from the adrenal glands to the immune cells to the neurochemical soup of the brain.

Cortisol, when left unchecked, is a direct enemy of muscle tissue. It promotes protein breakdown and inhibits muscle protein synthesis. Chronically elevated cortisol makes it harder to build muscle even when training and eating appropriately. This creates a grim loop: stress leads to muscle loss, which impairs resilience, which leads to more stress. Resistance training interrupts this loop by imposing a more useful kind of stress—one that produces recovery rather than erosion. It's not about reducing all stress; it's about replacing chaotic, unproductive stress with structured, adaptive stress.

This is also why lifting beats yoga or meditation when it comes to long-term stress regulation. While those modalities may reduce acute anxiety, they don't provoke physiological remodeling. They soothe, but they don't build. Strength training, by contrast, forces the body to adapt structurally and hormonally. It resets the feedback loops. And for aging adults who are often told to "take it easy" or "just go for a walk," this message is both outdated and harmful. Gentle activity is not sufficient to repair the damage done by chronic cortisol exposure. Intensity—appropriately scaled—is essential.

Psychologically, resistance training provides something no supplement or relaxation protocol can: a sense of agency. In a life stage where control seems to be slipping—over the body, over time, over outcomes—lifting introduces direct feedback. Load goes up. Reps increase. Movement improves. This sense of progression, of physical self-efficacy, counters the learned helplessness that often accompanies chronic stress and aging. A strong body is not just a physical asset. It is a psychological anchor.

There is also the neurological effect. Lifting stimulates the release of endorphins, dopamine, and brain-derived neurotrophic factor (BDNF)—all of which contribute to improved mood, cognition, and emotional regulation. But beyond the biochemistry, the process of lifting itself demands presence. You cannot ruminate while under a heavy barbell. You must breathe, brace, move. The mind is pulled out of abstract worry and into embodied action. This is not escapism. It is precision-grounded mindfulness, born not from stillness but from force production.

Many older adults assume that lifting might increase their stress because it's hard, foreign, or physically demanding. But that assumption misses the point. What lifting offers is not relaxation in the moment—it's transformation over time. It trains the nervous system to differentiate between real threat and imagined stress. It conditions the HPA axis to spike and recover, not hover in limbo. It puts cortisol in its place—not by eliminating it, but by making it earn its keep.

This matters because the long-term effects of chronic stress are not hypothetical. They are visible in bone scans, blood glucose charts, sleep trackers, and cognitive assessments. Stress accelerates every known pathway of aging: it frays telomeres, oxidizes tissue, impairs repair. And it often hides behind symptoms—fatigue, insomnia, weight gain—that get treated in isolation. What they often reflect, at root, is a regulatory system overrun by unmanaged hormonal noise. Resistance training is one of the few interventions that doesn't just dampen that noise—it retunes the entire system.

Cortisol is not the villain. Chronic, unmodulated cortisol is. And the solution is not to avoid stress, but to dose it with purpose. Strength training, properly applied, is stress therapy. It teaches the body how to respond, recover, and resist. It is structured adversity with a reward. It is the difference between being worn down by life and rising to meet it. You don't lift to escape stress. You lift to become the kind of person it can no longer unravel.

Chapter 24: Muscle and Cognitive Decline

Cognitive decline after midlife is typically framed as a problem of the brain alone—shrinking gray matter, fading neurotransmitters, compromised blood flow. But the story is incomplete. The brain does not age in isolation. It ages in the body, and the body, particularly its muscular system, plays a far greater role in preserving cognition than most people realize. Muscle is not just for movement. It is metabolically active, hormonally communicative, and deeply intertwined with neural health. Losing it doesn't just affect physical strength; it hastens cognitive decay. Conversely, building and maintaining muscle acts as a form of neuroprotection, particularly in adults over fifty, when both systems—muscular and cognitive—begin to erode in tandem unless challenged.

The link between muscle and mind begins with circulation. Skeletal muscle is a major driver of cardiovascular output. It doesn't just receive blood—it helps return it. Contracting muscle acts as a pump, enhancing venous return and improving systemic circulation. This directly influences cerebral blood flow. A brain that receives steady, forceful perfusion is a brain that maintains its function longer. Resistance training, by increasing cardiac stroke volume and vascular efficiency, supports this dynamic. It ensures the brain is not operating in a state of mild hypoxia, which over time erodes both memory and executive function.

But the connection goes deeper. Contracting muscles release myokines—biologically active molecules that communicate with distant tissues. Among these, irisin and cathepsin B stand out for their influence on the brain. These molecules cross the blood-brain barrier and stimulate the production of brain-derived neurotrophic factor (BDNF), a key regulator of neurogenesis, synaptic plasticity, and learning. BDNF is essentially brain fertilizer. It keeps neurons flexible, enhances signal transmission, and supports the growth of new connections. And it doesn't increase through crossword puzzles or fish oil. It increases through physical exertion, especially exertion against resistance.

This is not speculation. A 2012 study in *Archives of Internal Medicine* followed older women who performed resistance training twice weekly for a year. Compared to the control group, the lifters showed significantly improved executive function and memory scores, along with increased brain volume in regions associated with decision-making and emotional regulation. Other studies in *Neurobiology of Aging* and *The Journals of Gerontology* have demonstrated similar outcomes, with strength training outperforming stretching or balance exercises in preserving cognitive function. These aren't marginal benefits—they are structural changes in the brain's architecture, triggered by what happens in the glutes, hamstrings, and spine.

Strength also influences cognition through stability and autonomy. As balance deteriorates and falls become more common, older adults unconsciously begin to restrict movement. This reduces environmental engagement, social interaction, and sensory stimulation—all critical to cognitive maintenance. Weakness, therefore, doesn't just confine the body. It isolates the mind. It narrows experience and reduces the cognitive inputs that keep the brain adaptive. Strength training, by preserving physical confidence and capacity, maintains these broader forms of engagement. It enables older adults to live in their environment, not retreat from it.

There's also the hormonal dimension. Resistance training improves the body's regulation of cortisol, the primary stress hormone. Chronic stress is neurotoxic—it impairs memory, shrinks the hippocampus, and accelerates cognitive decline. By modulating the hypothalamic-pituitary-adrenal (HPA) axis, lifting weights helps regulate cortisol output, improving not just mood but the structural integrity of the brain. At the same time, lifting supports the anabolic hormones—testosterone, estrogen, IGF-1—that also influence brain function. Estrogen, for example, plays a key role in verbal memory, while testosterone impacts spatial reasoning and processing speed. These hormones decline with age, but resistance training helps preserve their signaling pathways, maintaining cognitive sharpness even in the absence of youthful hormone levels.

The neurological demands of lifting themselves also serve as training for the brain. Unlike steady-state cardio, which becomes automatic once a rhythm is established, strength training requires constant neuromuscular coordination. Every lift is a motor task: brace, align, stabilize, exert. Compound lifts like deadlifts, squats, and overhead presses require proprioception, balance, and fine-tuned control. They activate the cerebellum, basal ganglia, and prefrontal cortex in ways that reinforce motor learning and cognitive planning. The mind is not passive during a lift—it is solving problems under tension. Over time, this fortifies the neural circuits that protect against decline.

It's worth noting that the correlation between muscular strength and cognitive health isn't just associative—it's predictive. Large-scale longitudinal studies have found that lower grip strength and slower gait speed in midlife strongly predict dementia risk later in life. These aren't subtle trends. They're robust, dose-dependent relationships that hold even when controlling for age, education, and cardiovascular status. Weakness is not just a symptom of aging—it is a signpost of impending neurological regression. And unlike many brain biomarkers, strength can be measured cheaply, improved quickly, and maintained indefinitely.

The converse is also true. Muscle loss accelerates cognitive decline. Sarcopenia leads to metabolic instability, which worsens insulin sensitivity, which in turn impairs cerebrovascular health and promotes neuroinflammation. The brain, cut off from adequate nutrients and damaged by systemic inflammation, begins to downregulate. Memory slips. Focus wanes. Emotional regulation deteriorates. The tragic part is that these changes are often dismissed as "normal aging," when they are, in many cases, the downstream effect of preventable muscular atrophy.

Even sleep, a major pillar of cognitive preservation, is tied to muscle status. People who lift sleep deeper and more restoratively than their sedentary peers. This is not simply due to physical fatigue but to improved hormonal balance and circadian regulation. Better sleep consolidates memory, clears amyloid plaques, and repairs neuronal damage. It's a loop: strong bodies sleep better, which makes brains sharper, which facilitates better training, which makes bodies stronger. Remove muscle from that equation, and the loop collapses.

The implications are both urgent and hopeful. Urgent because the average adult loses about 1–2% of muscle mass per year after fifty without resistance training. Hopeful because that trajectory can be reversed. Muscle can be built, retained, and used to preserve cognitive vitality well into old age. There is no age at which strength training stops benefiting the brain. In fact, the later it's started, the more pronounced the benefits often are—because the contrast against baseline dysfunction is so stark.

Muscle is not just about posture, movement, or metabolism. It is about memory, identity, and selfhood. The loss of muscle is not merely the loss of physical capacity—it is the quiet erosion of the scaffolding that keeps the brain resilient. Cognitive decline is not inevitable, but without muscular intervention, it becomes probable. The brain needs challenge, blood flow, biochemical signaling, and protection from stress—all of which muscle provides. The deadlift and the dumbbell curl, though humble in appearance, are forms of cognitive therapy.

Aging gracefully is often presented as a matter of accepting decline. But this view ignores biology. The body and brain do not want to wither—they wither when no demand is placed on them. Strength is the demand. And from that demand, the mind responds: not with surrender, but with growth.

Chapter 25: The Anti-Fragile Aging Body

The conventional model of aging is built on caution. As the body grows older, advice trends toward mitigation: avoid impact, reduce intensity, stay safe. The assumption is that aging bodies are fragile—porcelain structures vulnerable to cracking under the strain of exertion. But this model is not only flawed; it's counterproductive. The truth is that the aging body, when exposed to appropriate stress, does not deteriorate—it adapts. Like muscle under load or bone under tension, it grows stronger through challenge. The goal is not merely to preserve what remains but to build a body that becomes more resilient under pressure. Not less breakable, but anti-fragile.

The concept of anti-fragility, popularized by Nassim Nicholas Taleb, describes systems that don't just resist stress but benefit from it. Muscles are a prime example. Subject them to load beyond their comfort zone and they respond by growing thicker, more coordinated, and metabolically sharper. Avoid stress, and they shrink. Bones follow the same principle—mechanical loading stimulates osteoblast activity, rebuilding the very scaffolding that keeps humans upright. The cardiovascular system, too, benefits from cyclical exertion. Exposure to strain, when followed by recovery, doesn't wear the system out—it tunes it.

Yet mainstream advice for those over fifty discourages such exposure. Risk aversion becomes the doctrine. Programs labeled "safe for seniors" tend to offer low-load, high-repetition fluff that fails to deliver any meaningful stimulus. The narrative becomes one of preservation rather than progress. But the data contradicts this narrative. A 2017 study in *Journal of Bone and Mineral Research* showed that older adults engaging in high-intensity resistance training—under supervision and with proper progression—gained strength, increased bone mineral density, and reduced fall risk more effectively than peers doing gentler modalities. Not only did they avoid injury—they reversed biological decline.

Anti-fragility in the aging body does not mean indiscriminate intensity. It means intentional exposure to stressors the body is capable of adapting to. It means progressive overload tailored to individual limits but not coddled by them. The load must be heavy enough to challenge tissue, the movements complex enough to demand coordination, and the recovery sufficient to consolidate the adaptation. There is no anti-fragility without friction. Challenge is the signal. Repair is the reward.

One of the most common arguments against loading older adults is the specter of injury. But the injury risk from lifting under control is dwarfed by the injury risk from falling due to weakness, or the slow-motion trauma of sarcopenia and metabolic disease. The sedentary lifestyle, marketed as prudence, is in fact a long, unbroken exposure to atrophy. It is a failure to provoke adaptation. And in the absence of challenge, systems decay. Muscles wither, bones thin, insulin sensitivity collapses, mitochondria shut down. The danger is not lifting—it's never lifting.

The anti-fragile body also resists psychological decline. Physical challenge reinforces confidence, agency, and a sense of momentum. Each successful session contradicts the story of decay. The bar gets heavier, but so does the resolve. For many adults over fifty, strength training is the first domain in which progress still feels possible. Weight is not symbolic—it's literal. It is something the body does not want to lift, but does anyway. Over time, this recalibrates how aging is perceived. Not as a retreat, but as a campaign.

There is also a neurological dimension to anti-fragility. Movement under load trains not just muscles but brains. Balance, proprioception, and neuromuscular recruitment all sharpen in response to physical demand. When the body is required to stabilize under load, the central nervous system adapts. This reduces fall risk, improves reaction times, and supports cognitive health. A frail body avoids the unexpected. An anti-fragile one becomes better at absorbing it.

Even inflammation, often thought to increase with training, declines over time with repeated exposure to resistance. Initially, acute inflammatory markers rise—a normal response to tissue disruption. But chronically, the body learns to resolve inflammation more efficiently. Interleukin profiles shift. C-reactive protein levels fall. The immune system becomes less reactive and more discriminating. The body, once trained, learns to protect itself without overreacting. It doesn't just endure stress—it learns from it.

This stands in stark contrast to the pharmacological model of aging, which treats symptoms in isolation. Blood pressure goes up? Take a pill. Bone density goes down? Prescribe bisphosphonates. Depression creeps in? Antidepressants. But none of these address the root issue: a system deprived of stimulus. Resistance training, when appropriately scaled, does not target a single system. It tunes the whole organism. It is polypharmacy through physiology. And unlike most medications, its benefits compound over time.

Critics of this approach argue that most older adults won't tolerate the discomfort of lifting heavy. That compliance is too low. That it's too late. But these arguments collapse under real-world data. Late-life lifters consistently report increased energy, confidence, autonomy, and even joy. Compliance improves not because the workouts are easy, but because they are meaningful. The body is not designed for endless maintenance—it is designed for adaptation. And when given the chance, it adapts far more readily than most expect.

Importantly, anti-fragility requires recovery. Stress without rest is damage. But rest without stress is decay. The balance matters. Older lifters need more recovery, not less training. The training must be dense, not frequent. Shorter sessions, longer rests, better sleep. Nutrition must support repair—sufficient protein, micronutrient sufficiency, and total caloric adequacy. But once these elements are in place, the aging body is not a liability. It is an engine. Just one that has to be warmed up before pushed.

The final lie about aging is that it's only about loss. Loss of strength, speed, libido, vitality. But loss is not the baseline—it is the result of neglect. Strength is not preserved by default. Neither is balance, bone density, or cognition. These must be challenged to be retained. They must be demanded from the body repeatedly. Anti-fragility is not magical thinking. It's biological realism. Adaptation does not retire at fifty. It just charges more interest.

In practical terms, this means the standard exercise prescription for older adults needs to be rewritten. Replace "gentle" with "progressive." Replace "safe" with "meaningful." Replace "low-impact" with "appropriate intensity." The aging body is not a glass figurine. It is a living system capable of regeneration—if given the right type of demand. And that demand does not need to be heroic. It just needs to be enough to provoke repair.

Aging cannot be avoided, but fragility can. The body will respond to the stories we tell it. If we tell it to retreat, it will shrink. If we tell it to rise, it will build. The anti-fragile body is not born of genetics or supplements. It is built—under load, under pressure, one deliberate rep at a time.

Chapter 26: Sleep and Recovery in Older Lifters

Sleep is often framed as a passive act, the reward after a day's exertion. But in the physiology of an aging lifter, sleep is not a luxury—it is anabolic infrastructure. Recovery is not what happens when you stop training; it is the continuation of adaptation in a different hormonal context. And after fifty, that context changes. Circadian rhythms drift. Melatonin declines. Sleep becomes lighter, more fragmented, and more vulnerable to stress. At the same time, the stakes rise. Recovery isn't just about feeling refreshed—it's about preserving the gains that keep you out of decline. In older lifters, sleep is the second workout. It's where the real rebuilding happens.

Muscle recovery is primarily driven by sleep-dependent hormonal cascades. Deep sleep, particularly slow-wave sleep, is when growth hormone pulses most strongly. In youth, this system is robust. But with age, slow-wave sleep shrinks, and so do the associated anabolic signals. Without deliberate sleep optimization, even well-executed training plans begin to falter. Progress stalls, fatigue lingers, and soreness overextends its welcome. The body doesn't lack motivation—it lacks repair.

This matters because the act of lifting weights, while essential, is catabolic in the moment. It breaks tissue down, depletes glycogen, provokes inflammation, and disrupts homeostasis. The benefit of training doesn't occur in the gym; it occurs in the recovery window that follows. And in adults over fifty, that window must be treated with more care than in earlier decades. Younger lifters can get away with short nights and erratic schedules. Older lifters cannot. The margin for adaptation shrinks, and recovery becomes the rate-limiting step in progress.

Cortisol plays a central role here. Chronically elevated cortisol—whether from stress, under-recovery, or disrupted sleep—competes directly with anabolic hormones like testosterone, growth hormone, and IGF-1. It increases protein breakdown, blunts hypertrophy, and impairs glucose metabolism. Poor sleep drives cortisol up, setting the stage for muscle loss and fat gain, even in the presence of solid training and nutrition. It's the invisible saboteur. You can lift and eat with textbook precision, but if your sleep is fractured, your results will reflect exhaustion, not effort.

Sleep also regulates appetite through the leptin-ghrelin axis. Sleep deprivation lowers leptin (the satiety hormone) and raises ghrelin (the hunger hormone), making it harder to regulate caloric intake and easier to overeat—especially high-carbohydrate foods. In older adults whose metabolism is already more insulin resistant and whose muscle mass is harder to preserve, this becomes a problem of compounding losses. Poor sleep leads to poor eating, which leads to poor recovery, which leads to stagnation or decline despite hours in the gym.

Insufficient or poor-quality sleep also impairs coordination, balance, and reaction time. These are not cosmetic deficits—they directly impact injury risk. An aging body with compromised sleep is slower to respond, more prone to missteps, and less resilient to minor disruptions. Resistance training improves neuromuscular efficiency, but only if the nervous system gets the rest it needs to rewire and stabilize new motor patterns. Skimp on sleep, and those gains get erased before they're consolidated.

So what does sleep optimization look like for older lifters? It's not about more hours in bed—it's about deeper, more efficient sleep architecture. That starts with consistency. The circadian system thrives on regularity, and the older it gets, the more it resists irregularity. A consistent bedtime and wake-up time— even on weekends—is foundational. Sleep hygiene matters: dark room, cool temperature, no screens an hour before bed. These aren't trivial habits. They are the environmental conditions for growth hormone release, mitochondrial repair, and central nervous system recalibration.

Alcohol, often tolerated in youth with minimal consequence, becomes a sleep disruptor in middle age. Even small amounts reduce REM sleep and increase nighttime awakenings. Similarly, caffeine lingers longer in older adults due to slower hepatic clearance. A coffee at noon might still be interfering with deep sleep at midnight. These are not moral considerations—they are biochemical facts. If the goal is recovery, the inputs must support the output.

Training timing also affects sleep. Late-night high-intensity sessions can elevate heart rate and core temperature for hours, delaying sleep onset and reducing sleep depth. Morning or early-afternoon sessions tend to align better with circadian rhythms, allowing the body to cool down and settle into the parasympathetic state required for restful sleep. But this isn't a fixed rule. Individual variance matters. Some lifters sleep better after evening sessions. The key is to monitor how sleep responds—not to follow blanket prescriptions.

Napping, once dismissed as lazy, becomes a strategic tool in older lifters. A 20- to 30-minute nap in the early afternoon can significantly boost alertness and improve recovery markers without interfering with nighttime sleep. It's not a substitute for overnight rest, but a supplement—especially on training days or after poor sleep. It helps manage systemic fatigue, improve mood, and lower cortisol. Again, it's not about indulgence—it's about biological efficiency.

Nutrition also plays a role. Evening meals should include sufficient protein to support overnight muscle protein synthesis, ideally with slow-digesting sources like casein. Carbohydrates in the evening, contrary to outdated dogma, can actually improve sleep onset and depth by increasing tryptophan availability and serotonin synthesis. The old advice to avoid eating at night overlooks the reality that recovery does not clock out at 6 p.m. The aging lifter needs a different rulebook—one informed by adaptation, not austerity.

Sleep supplements can help, but should be used judiciously. Melatonin, in low doses, can assist in resetting circadian drift, especially in older adults whose natural production declines. Magnesium and glycine have mild calming effects and may improve sleep onset and quality. But reliance on pills without addressing underlying behavioral factors misses the point. The goal is not sedation—it's recovery. That requires a systemwide approach, not just another bottle on the nightstand.

Finally, it's essential to reframe rest as productive. In a culture that valorizes grind and hustle, rest gets mistaken for laziness. But in the physiology of strength, rest is the phase of remodeling. Muscles don't grow in the gym. They grow in the hours after, when the immune system clears debris, when protein is synthesized, when neurons rewire. For older lifters, these processes take longer—but they still happen. Progress doesn't stop after fifty. It just demands more patience, more precision, and more respect for the unseen half of the training equation.

Training hard without recovering hard is not discipline—it's negligence. The body over fifty cannot be forced. It must be coaxed. Sleep is how that coaxing happens. It is the lever that turns effort into adaptation. Neglect it, and you're not training—you're simply eroding, one sleepless night at a time.

Chapter 27: Why Machines Are Better Than Nothing

Free weights are often fetishized in fitness culture, held up as the gold standard of resistance training—complex, "functional," raw. Machines, by contrast, are dismissed as inferior: too easy, too guided, too forgiving. But this dichotomy is not just elitist—it's physiologically wrong, and practically harmful, especially for older lifters. Past fifty, the goal is not to mimic the training of twenty-something athletes. It is to rebuild tissue, preserve function, and extend independence. In that context, machines are not just acceptable—they are often the ideal point of entry. They offer a scalable, joint-friendly, neurologically accessible path to strength that avoids the common pitfalls of intimidation, instability, and injury.

By design, machines constrain movement through a fixed path. Critics argue this limits joint recruitment and core engagement.

What they fail to appreciate is that these constraints are exactly what make machines safe and effective for deconditioned or mobility-restricted lifters. The seated chest press, for example, removes the balance and scapular control required in a barbell bench press, allowing the lifter to focus purely on generating force. For someone with shoulder pathology, this isn't dumbing down the movement—it's removing unnecessary risk. The machine doesn't replace free weights; it enables the lifter to train around limitations without sacrificing stimulus.

Strength gains in aging populations aren't about mastering complex Olympic lifts—they're about applying sufficient tension to muscle tissue consistently. Machines allow that with less neural fatigue, less technical failure, and less risk of compensatory movement patterns. A 2014 randomized controlled trial in *The Journal of Aging and Physical Activity* found that older adults using resistance machines three times a week for 12 weeks improved strength, balance, and functional capacity just as significantly as a free-weight group, with fewer reported joint complaints. The mechanisms of adaptation—mechanical tension, progressive overload, metabolic stress—don't care if the resistance comes from iron plates, cables, or a gleaming circuit machine. Muscles respond to load, not ideology.

Machines also allow easier autoregulation. On days when sleep, stress, or joint flare-ups impair readiness, adjusting load on a selectorized machine takes seconds. There is no need to warm up with the bar, rack plates, or coordinate spotters. For older adults juggling unpredictable energy levels, this ease of use increases compliance. And in training, compliance beats idealism. A perfect program followed inconsistently is less effective than a good-enough plan executed with discipline. Machines lower the barrier to entry and raise the floor of consistency. That alone makes them indispensable.

Neurological efficiency also matters. Complex barbell lifts demand coordination, proprioception, and motor patterning that may not come easily to beginners in their sixties. Machines reduce the cognitive load. They simplify movement to its essential muscular task: exert force. For older adults with no athletic background—or those re-entering training after decades away—this reduction in complexity improves confidence and control. Over time, some may graduate to free weights. Others may not. In both cases, progress is still made.

Moreover, joint constraints in aging lifters aren't theoretical— they're anatomical. Decades of accumulated wear, past injuries, arthritis, or surgeries create limitations that free-weight movements often aggravate. A low-bar squat may be ideal in textbooks, but for someone with degenerative lumbar discs or knee osteoarthritis, it may be inaccessible or even dangerous. A leg press or hack squat machine allows the same muscle groups to be trained with less spinal loading and better control of range of motion. These are not compromises—they're intelligent adaptations. Machines aren't cheating. They're problem-solving.

There is also a psychological dimension to machine training. Intimidation is real. Walking into a gym filled with clanging barbells, athletic twenty-somethings, and incomprehensible equipment can be paralyzing for the uninitiated. Machines, with their simple diagrams, pin-loaded weight stacks, and intuitive design, reduce that barrier. They provide structure where confusion would otherwise reign. This matters, because nothing sabotages consistency like fear of looking incompetent. Machines offer early success, which builds confidence, which sustains motivation. And in the psychology of aging, belief in the ability to improve is often half the battle.

Some argue that machines don't train "functional" movement patterns. But that claim collapses under scrutiny. The purpose of training isn't to simulate real-world motion with perfect fidelity—it's to build the raw materials of function: strength, mobility, endurance, stability. Once those are developed, transfer to daily activities occurs naturally. The leg extension does not mimic climbing stairs, but it strengthens the quadriceps that power that motion. A cable row doesn't look like picking up groceries, but it reinforces the pulling musculature that prevents shoulder dysfunction. Function is not a movement pattern—it's a capacity.

In rehabilitation contexts, machines are often the only safe point of re-entry. After a joint replacement, fracture, or major surgery, balance and proprioception may be too compromised to manage free-weight training. Machines provide external stability, allowing loading to resume earlier in the recovery process. This protects against the muscular atrophy that typically follows long periods of immobilization. They don't just maintain—they accelerate return to function by reintroducing stress at a tolerable level.

And for those managing chronic disease—osteoporosis, cardiovascular issues, diabetes—machines offer a safer, more modifiable environment to train without compromising safety. Blood pressure spikes can be managed with semi-recumbent machines. Bone loading can be scaled precisely without risking falls. Neuropathy, poor vision, or vestibular issues can be worked around rather than used as an excuse to remain inactive. Machines are not the consolation prize—they are a scalable tool for progress when biology becomes more demanding.

Are machines perfect? No. They limit proprioceptive challenge and often isolate muscles more than compound free-weight lifts. But that doesn't make them useless. It makes them context-dependent. For advanced trainees with full mobility and years under the bar, free weights may offer superior long-term adaptability. But for the vast majority of older adults—those starting late, recovering from injury, or managing chronic conditions—machines deliver stimulus without unnecessary risk. And most importantly, they get people to train.

The best program is the one you can sustain. And the best equipment is the one you'll actually use. If machines provide the foothold that keeps you coming back, then they are not secondary—they are essential. Dismissing them as inferior is like criticizing a walker for not being a sprint—missing the point entirely. The goal after fifty is not to impress anyone with training purity. It's to retain strength, reclaim function, and add years to the timeline of independence.

Machines may not build world champions. But they rebuild lives. And in the second half of life, that's the only kind of strength that matters.

Chapter 28: The One Rep You Can't Skip: Getting Off the Floor

Among all the strength benchmarks that matter past fifty—deadlift, squat, overhead press—none is more predictive of survival than the ability to get up off the floor without assistance. It is a deceptively simple task, one that most people don't think about until they can't do it. But physiologically, it's a full-spectrum challenge. It tests leg strength, hip mobility, core control, proprioception, and balance—all at once. And the inability to perform this movement isn't just a sign of physical decline. It's a signal of lost autonomy. The floor is where weakness is exposed in its rawest form. And getting off it is, quite literally, a rehearsal for staying alive.

A 2012 study published in the *European Journal of Preventive Cardiology* made this correlation unambiguous. Researchers tracked over 2,000 adults aged 51 to 80 and assessed their ability to sit and rise from the floor without using their hands, knees, or other supports. Those who struggled—who needed multiple points of contact—were significantly more likely to die over the study period, regardless of weight, age, or cardiovascular status. The lower the score on this seemingly simple task, the higher the all-cause mortality risk. The test wasn't about fitness in the gym—it was about whether a person could survive in their own home.

This movement isn't just about strength in isolation—it's about integrated strength. It requires the ability to coordinate upper and lower body segments, to stabilize the trunk while the legs drive extension, and to balance dynamically through shifting weight. It's a strength problem, a control problem, and a coordination problem, all layered into one. And each of those problems is magnified with age, not because the movement becomes harder, but because the body has been deconditioned by decades of chair dependence, sedentarism, and fear of falling.

Yet it's precisely this fear—of falling and not being able to rise—that underpins why this ability is so critical. In older adults, the risk of fall-related injury is not confined to the moment of impact. It extends to the aftermath. An uninjured but stranded adult, unable to rise, faces a cascade of risks: hypothermia, dehydration, rhabdomyolysis, pressure ulcers, even death. The physiological act of standing is therefore not just functional—it's protective. It is emergency preparedness disguised as a mobility test.

The muscles most responsible for this movement—glutes, hamstrings, quads, abdominals, spinal erectors—are the same ones most neglected in untrained older adults. They atrophy silently, often under the guise of "aging," until one day the floor becomes a trap instead of a surface. The tragedy is that this decline is not inevitable. It is simply unchallenged. Most adults never train the full pattern of sitting down and standing back up without supports. They practice partial ranges—squats to chairs, lunges to cushions—but rarely the full, unsupported motion from ground to vertical. And because they don't train it, they lose it.

Strength training reclaims this movement in both direct and indirect ways. Directly, by programming ground-based transitions—Turkish get-ups, roll-to-stands, deep bodyweight squats, and eccentric floor descents. Indirectly, by building the raw physical resources—hip extension power, spinal rigidity, trunk rotation—that the movement draws upon. And while these capacities can be built with free weights, machines, or bodyweight, the crucial element is intent: to train the pattern, not just the parts.

This task also reveals the importance of eccentric control—something often neglected in standard programs. Getting down to the floor gracefully is as important as getting up from it. Older adults who lack eccentric strength in the hips and knees tend to crash downward, rather than descend with control. This not only increases fall risk but makes the movement harder to reverse. Controlled descents, loaded step-downs, and split squats teach the body to yield without surrendering tension. Without this, even a trained lifter can struggle to reorient from prone to standing if they haven't trained the intermediate phases.

It's also a balance problem. Getting off the floor challenges the vestibular system, ankle stability, and the body's ability to shift center of gravity without collapsing. These are not theoretical concerns. In real-world scenarios, especially after a trip or slip, the ability to pivot from supine or side-lying to kneeling to standing is a literal life skill. No piece of equipment can substitute for it. It must be trained on the ground, under one's own bodyweight, repeatedly and with progressive complexity.

The movement also carries psychological weight. The inability to rise without help signals, for many, the loss of agency. It often precedes the move to assisted living, the hiring of in-home care, or the cessation of independent travel. It erodes confidence long before it impairs performance. The floor, once a neutral space, becomes something to avoid. But when this task is re-trained—when the floor is reclaimed—it often has an outsized impact on self-perception. Independence returns. Risk tolerance increases. Life opens up.

It is worth noting that while strength is the primary requirement, mobility is a close second. Stiff hips, fused ankles, and kyphotic thoracic spines make the sit-to-stand transition unnecessarily difficult. This is not just about muscle—it's about movement quality. Regular strength training that incorporates full-range patterns, mobility work under load, and isometric control improves these prerequisites. Mobility gained passively is often temporary. Mobility earned under tension sticks.

Training to get off the floor doesn't require exotic programming. It requires prioritization. It belongs in warm-ups, in conditioning circuits, in cool-downs. Not just for athletes, but especially for those who feel furthest from athleticism. The irony is that the further one is from this ability, the more essential its training becomes. And unlike maximal deadlifts or hypertrophy thresholds, this movement is binary: either you can do it, or you can't. There is no workaround. No modification. The floor is indifferent to excuses.

For coaches and clinicians, this movement should be a screening tool. Before prescribing another round of cardio or another stretch for tight hamstrings, ask: can this person get up off the floor without help? If not, strength must become the first prescription—not for aesthetics, not even for health metrics, but for safety and survival. Because in real life, the only rep that matters is the one that gets you back up.

Getting off the floor is not a parlor trick. It is a daily referendum on whether your training is serving you. It integrates what matters—power, coordination, mobility, control—into one unsparing test. And it's not just a measure of how strong you are. It's a prediction of how long you'll remain on your own.

Chapter 29: No, It's Not Too Late

One of the most persistent, quietly corrosive beliefs in aging populations is that the window for transformation has closed. Strength? Too late. Muscle? That ship has sailed. Functional independence? Accept its decline. This narrative is not merely wrong—it's biologically illiterate. The human body remains responsive to strength training well into the eighth and even ninth decade. Muscle is not a youthful gift—it's a conditional response to load, at any age. The only real expiration date is the one imposed by inaction. And the science is unequivocal: it is never too late to build strength, reverse decline, and reclaim agency over one's own body.

Late-life lifters do not need to match their younger selves to make progress. The physiology of adaptation may slow with age, but it does not shut off. Muscle protein synthesis still occurs. Neuromuscular coordination still improves. Bone density still responds to load. The rates may be diminished, but the capacity remains. A 2021 meta-analysis in *Sports Medicine* reviewed over 50 studies on resistance training in adults over 60 and found consistent gains in strength, muscle mass, and physical function—even in participants starting from a completely untrained state. Some of the most dramatic improvements came from individuals in their seventies and eighties.

There is no clearer refutation of the "too late" myth than the lives of those who started lifting after fifty and changed their trajectory entirely. Take Sy Perlis, who began lifting in his sixties and set a world bench press record in his nineties. Or Ernestine Shepherd, who didn't touch a dumbbell until she was 56 and became a competitive bodybuilder. These aren't freaks of nature—they are individuals who simply replaced resignation with repetition. Their results weren't magic. They were the result of simple, progressive overload applied consistently across time. The kind of results available to anyone willing to begin.

Even individuals with severe mobility limitations, chronic disease, or long sedentary histories can improve. Resistance training in populations with type 2 diabetes, osteoarthritis, and even heart failure has been shown not only to be safe but therapeutically superior to pharmacological interventions in some cases. A 2019 study in *The Journals of Gerontology* demonstrated that frail older adults, including those in assisted living, improved gait speed, grip strength, and functional independence through supervised resistance programs. Again and again, the research points in one direction: decline is not destiny. Strength is not reserved for the young.

Starting late often comes with psychological baggage—shame, fear, self-doubt. The gym is seen as the terrain of the already-fit, the young, the unbroken. But this perception does not match reality. The real training floor includes people rehabbing joint replacements, managing chronic pain, and restarting after decades of inactivity. And the truth is, late-life lifters often bring qualities younger trainees lack: patience, discipline, and a deeper appreciation of what strength actually means. They are not chasing aesthetics or numbers. They are chasing the ability to live fully.

Physiologically, older adults often respond surprisingly well to training. The neuromuscular system, even after long dormancy, can be reactivated. Muscle memory—technically myonuclear permanence—allows previously trained muscles to rebound faster, even after years of detraining. Tendons and ligaments, while slower to adapt, do respond to progressive loading and regain elasticity and stiffness over time. Bone density, often thought to decline irreversibly, can be maintained or even increased through high-intensity resistance training. It's not about becoming indestructible. It's about becoming capable again.

For those afraid of injury, it's worth noting that injury risk from resistance training in older adults is remarkably low—especially when compared to the risk of falling, metabolic disease, or disuse atrophy. The most dangerous thing an aging person can do is to remain weak. Functional incapacity, not heavy lifting, is what sends people into long-term care. Sarcopenia and its companions—frailty, insulin resistance, poor balance—are the true risks. And the only proven antidote is strength.

The notion that late training yields only marginal benefit also misunderstands how dramatic even small improvements can be. A modest gain in quadriceps strength can turn a two-handed struggle up the stairs into a one-hand ascent. A few more pounds on a deadlift can mean the difference between lifting a suitcase or calling for help. Independence isn't won by massive PRs. It's won by micro-revolutions—each rep a vote against decline.

Resistance training also impacts cognitive function, mood, and resilience. Depression, common in older populations, is blunted by the biochemical and psychological effects of lifting. Dopamine, serotonin, and brain-derived neurotrophic factor increase. Executive function improves. Memory stabilizes. Training is not just for the body—it is a scaffold for the mind. And when an older adult begins to see progress—increased energy, better posture, easier movement—the effects ripple outward into every domain of life.

Starting later also forces smarter training. Older lifters learn quickly that recovery matters more than volume, that mobility can't be ignored, and that the ego must be subordinated to progress. They train with focus rather than frenzy. The result is often cleaner technique, better compliance, and fewer injuries. Late starters are not handicapped—they are often the most consistent athletes in the gym.

For coaches, clinicians, and family members, the message must be clear: never assume someone is "too old" to start lifting. The threshold for progress is low, the tools are available, and the benefits are profound. What they need is not perfect programming or specialized equipment. They need exposure to load, scaled appropriately, and encouragement grounded in evidence, not pity. Muscle can be built in a nursing home. Deadlifts can be trained with a kettlebell. Functional movement can be restored in a garage. It's not the environment that matters—it's the exposure.

The tragedy is not aging. It's surrender. The belief that nothing can be done is far more toxic than any physical limitation. And yet, when people finally start—even if they begin at 60, 70, or 80—they almost always say the same thing: "I wish I had started sooner." But that regret is not a curse. It's a signal. And it's followed by the realization that "sooner" is now. Because once the first rep is completed, the clock doesn't reverse—but the direction of decline does.

There will always be reasons to hesitate. Time. Pain. Fatigue. Intimidation. But the truth is simple: it is not too late. Not for strength. Not for muscle. Not for capacity. The body, regardless of age, listens to the signals it receives. And when that signal is deliberate tension, challenged limits, and consistent effort, the response is clear. It builds. Slowly, stubbornly, and unmistakably—it builds.

Chapter 30: Train for Life, Not the Mirror

The mirror has long been the altar of fitness culture—abs carved into submission, biceps inflated for admiration, physiques curated not for function but for spectacle. It's a seductive, photogenic fantasy. But past fifty, that fantasy collapses under the weight of biology. Aesthetics, if they happen, are a side effect—not a goal. The goal is survival. The goal is independence. The goal is to retain the ability to rise from the floor, carry groceries, walk without hesitation, sleep through the night, and live without a constant undercurrent of fear that the body will betray you. Training after fifty is not about how you look. It's about whether you can keep living the way you want to.

The aging body does not stop adapting—it stops being asked to. When muscles shrink, balance falters, and bones become brittle, it isn't because the body gave up. It's because the environment became too soft, too easy, too sedentary. Muscles need load. Bones need impact. The nervous system needs complexity. Training provides those missing ingredients. It restores stimulus where there was only entropy. But the training must be chosen for its function, not its reflection. The abs you want will not save you from a fall. The visible veins in your forearms won't carry your luggage. Strength, on the other hand, will. It is the currency of continued autonomy.

Much of mainstream fitness media sells the idea that you should continue to chase the body of your youth. Tighter, leaner, more defined. But for those over fifty, this pursuit often backfires. Crash dieting cannibalizes muscle. Excessive cardio wears down joints. Chasing low body fat without support erodes energy and hormone balance. The body becomes lighter but not stronger. And what's lost—lean mass, bone density, recovery capacity—is rarely recovered without structured resistance training. The mirror may reward you in the short term, but it does nothing to prevent sarcopenia, osteopenia, or insulin resistance. Training for life means resisting the urge to make every decision based on visibility.

The body does not respond to your preferences. It responds to demand. Lifting heavy things—consistently, progressively, and with intention—tells the body to retain what matters. That message becomes more urgent as you age. Every year after fifty, the baseline of muscle mass and strength drops unless you intervene. And once strength falls below the threshold needed for daily life, it's not aesthetics that disappear—it's freedom. That's why the real transformation isn't physical—it's existential. It's the moment you realize that training is no longer a hobby. It's a form of resistance against decline.

This reframing is not defeatist—it's liberating. Because once the chase for perfection is replaced by the pursuit of resilience, training becomes sustainable. You no longer measure success by the mirror, but by metrics that matter: how much you can lift, how fast you recover, how easily you can get off the floor, how confidently you can move through space. These are not superficial milestones. They are predictive markers of mortality and morbidity. Grip strength, for example, is a better predictor of cardiovascular death than systolic blood pressure. The mirror never gave you that data. The barbell does.

Training for life also means training through life's interruptions. Joint pain, surgeries, illnesses, stress—these are not reasons to stop, but variables to adjust for. The mirror punishes inconsistency. But strength adapts to what it's given. It meets you where you are, provided you show up. You might lift less, move slower, or train less frequently during difficult seasons, but you still train. Because the alternative is regression. The older you get, the steeper the slope becomes. Coasting is no longer an option. Maintenance is movement. Movement is maintenance.

It also means training for the things that never show up in selfies—balance, stability, power, grip, gait speed. The world is full of surfaces that aren't flat, of loads that aren't even, of tasks that aren't planned. Training with complexity, unpredictability, and functional variety prepares you for this uncertainty. And this preparation doesn't have an expiration date. You can train for better balance at 70. You can regain lost strength at 80. You can improve power output in your 90s. Not to impress anyone—but to protect yourself. Aesthetics don't protect you from the floor. Functional strength does.

Those who train past midlife also understand something that younger lifters often don't: training is a privilege. When peers are on prescription cocktails, undergoing surgeries, or retreating from their bodies entirely, you are showing up to deliberately challenge yours. That act is defiance in its most useful form. It says: decline is not inevitable. It's conditional. And the condition is this—you stop asking your body to perform.

This doesn't mean you must chase personal records into your sixties. It means you prioritize consistency over intensity, progression over volume, quality over quantity. You don't train harder—you train smarter. You accept that recovery takes longer, that joints need more warm-up, that mobility requires intention. But none of that diminishes the training. In fact, it elevates it. Because training with wisdom is how you keep training at all.

There will still be days when you catch a glimpse of yourself and wish for the body you had at thirty. That's natural. But with experience comes a sharper lens. You'll begin to notice different signs of progress: how you walked across the room without pain. How you lifted your grandchild effortlessly. How you carried your suitcase up the stairs instead of waiting for an escalator. These are victories the mirror will never show—but your life will reflect them in every moment you move unassisted.

Training for life means choosing dignity over vanity. It means understanding that muscle is not for admiration—it's for survival. That strength is not a vanity metric—it's a vital sign. And that the act of training is not self-improvement—it is self-preservation. You're not sculpting a statue. You're reinforcing a structure that needs to last decades longer than your reflection.

Eventually, the mirror stops cooperating. Even the best genetics fade. Skin loosens, angles soften, lighting stops helping. But the barbell doesn't care. The kettlebell doesn't care. The body, surprisingly, doesn't care. It will still respond to load. It will still build muscle. It will still grow stronger. Not to look better—but to live better. And that is the only form of transformation that truly endures.

Train for life. Not for a beach photo. Not for a compliment. Not for Instagram. Train so that when you're eighty-five and standing at the top of a staircase, your body knows exactly what to do next. And does it, without hesitation.

Disclaimer

The information in this book is provided for educational and informational purposes only and is not intended as medical advice. Neither the author nor Southerland Publishing is a medical professional. You should always consult a qualified health care provider before beginning any new diet, exercise program, supplement regimen, or treatment plan. Reliance on any content in this book is solely at your own risk. Southerland Publishing and the author disclaim all liability for any injuries, losses, or damages that may arise from the use or misuse of the information contained herein. Seek personalized guidance from a licensed practitioner for your unique health needs.

Made in the USA
Monee, IL
05 July 2025

20558705R00085